Relationships: A Bridge or a Burden?

George M. Matthews II

Relationships: A Bridge or a Burden?
by George M. Matthews II

Printed in the United States of America

Library of Congress Control Number: 2002100980
ISBN 1-931232-96-2

Xulon Press
11350 Random Hills Road
Suite 800
Fairfax, VA 22030
(703) 279-6511
XulonPress.com

Contents

Introduction

I want to define the word "relationship." A relationship is a personal connection to another individual by blood, marriage, sexual intercourse, or association. The word "connected" means to join or fasten; to link together or to reach a thing aimed at. You may have been reaching at certain things that should not have been your aim, but you reached them and now you are in a "relationship." You may be trying to figure out, "How did I get here?"

Let me also give you a definition of the word "fellowship." It means friendly association; harmonious flow; a mutual sharing, as in an experience, activity, or interest. A relationship that operates properly must be based on and centered around fellowship.

In this book, I will spend some time discussing "relationships" since everyone is not married nor desires to be married, but everyone is in some type of relationship. For some of you, that is a revelation; for some, encouragement; for others, bad news. God has not ordained everyone to be married, but he has ordained for all to be in a relationship. Marriage is an option, a choice. It is not a commandment. You do not have to be married. The criterion for determining whether or not God has called you to be married is having those little feelings, emotions, and sensitivity as it relates to a person of the opposite gender. Proper relationship or association with others is not optional but rather it is mandatory for the success God has intended.

One thing to consider when we talk about the subject of marriage and other associations is your spiritual foundation. What is the center or foundation of your marital relationship? If the Word of God is not the center, you are headed to divorce court. You are headed to the lonely hearts club. You are headed to having your feelings hurt. By "center" I mean that you and the other person involved sit down and look at the Bible when you have problems. If you do not do this, you will be headed nowhere.

Humans in and of themselves do not know how to relate to each other. That is why some men physically abuse women. Men do not know how to relate to women without the Word of God. Some men get the Word and still knock on women. I remember when I was about seven or eight years old, I kicked my sister. My dad, who is a pastor and has been for many years, heard what I had done and called me into his room, and my sister came also, crying. She had annoyed me, and I had asked her repeatedly to leave me alone (you know how it is with children) and she would not do it. So I put a "stompin" on her. I kicked the cookies out of her, and my dad kicked the cookies out of me with his belt. From that day to this one, I have not put my foot on a woman again. I believe if men are disciplined and taught by their parents when they are young, much of this problem of abuse wouldn't exist. Many parents have "missed it" when people are physically or verbally abusive to others. Abuse simply means to take unfair advantage of a relationship.

I told my wife before we got married that whatever challenges we have, we would not scar each other over them. I said to her that if she feels she cannot live with me in peace, we will have to separate until peace comes back into the house, and we will have "to do what we have to do." We will not fight and knock each other around. I will be able to go to sleep in my house, and not with one eye open and one eye closed. I will not have to worry about going to sleep. I just won't deal with that, praise the Lord.

As you read this book, I pray the wisdom, insight, and direction of God necessary to build strong relationships, homes, and businesses will flood every area of your human spirit.

Preface

═══════════════════════════════

This book is designed to be a manual for developing and maintaining productive, viable relationships. May its contents serve as a tool for detecting attributes capable of promoting desirable associations. The opposite end of this spectrum also is very necessary. In many instances, one may be involved in alliances that previously were beneficial, but as time progresses, find themselves no longer benefitting. God's word provides insight into this sometimes agonizing ordeal.

I believe God's will for man is contained in Genesis 1:26, **"And God said, Let us (the Godhead trinity) make man in our image, after our likeness: and let them have dominion over the fish of the sea, and over the fowl of the air, and over the cattle, and over __all__ the earth, and over every creeping thing that creepeth upon the earth."** As you can see, God uses the pronoun "us" to describe a "relationship" of more than one personality being imbued into man's being. He (God) also uses three words—image, likeness, and dominion—to express in clear detail His intention for man's success. The word image in this context means:

- *a copy*
- *representative or likeness*
- *a statue*
- ***an idea or representation of anything of the mind***

- *to copy by the imagination*

This "success," however, would be predicated upon a correct relationship with the Creator. This would lead to a meaningful and significant interaction with mankind, promoting a winsome climate in all man sets forth to accomplish. Now we can see clearly that when Satan set out to become the enemy of God (Isaiah 14:12), it was relationship that was truly at the center of the attack.

CHAPTER I

God's Will Is to Give You Rest

In an attempt to address the revelation God shared with me regarding relationships, it is important that we recognize that all God has intended for man will be disclosed through a relationship of some type or another. There are many different types of relationships one can enter: marital, family, platonic, church, social, and business are just a few. The purpose of this book is to provide insight into the selection and maintenance of relationships. In the chapters to follow, I will rely upon marital and male/female associations as examples to more clearly support the information given. I use these types of relationships because it seems all humans can readily relate to the challenges associated with the male/female factor. St. Mark 4:2 (amplified) states, "And He taught them many things in parables (illustrations or comparisons put beside truths to explain them) . . . . " So you see, it is in keeping with the manner of Jesus' teaching style to use examples to clarify certain truths.

Let's begin talking about our subject, Relationships: A Bridge or A Burden? Some of you are in correct relationships and they are a bridge to you, and yet others of you are in incorrect relationships and they are a burden. While praying one day, the Lord said to me that relationships are either of the two. He said, "I ordained relationships to be a bridge, not a burden."

In St. Matthew 11:28, Jesus says, "Come unto me all ye that

labor and are heavy laden, and I will give you rest. Take my yoke upon you and learn of me, for I am meek and lowly in heart, and ye shall find rest unto your souls. For my yoke is easy and my burden is light." The New Life version of the Bible translates it this way: "Come to me all of you who work and have heavy loads; I will give you rest. Follow my teachings and learn from me. I am gentle and do not have pride. You will have rest for your souls . . . ."

From our relationships, we are supposed to achieve rest for our minds. A relationship for me, as a child of God, is supposed to produce *rest* to my mind, *rest* to my body, and *rest* to my spirit. Listen to the remainder of this translation, ". . . for my way of carrying a load is easy, and my load is not heavy." Prior to entering into any relationship, whether it is a family, parental, erotic, philos (brotherly), conjugal, business, employment, or friendly one, God says you generally come into that relationship with a heavy load of some type. It is heavy because you are the only one carrying it. Now it is supposed to be lighter because there is someone else with you who should be sharing the load. Would you agree that when two people share one load, it is lighter? The Bible says that a three-fold cord is not quickly (easily) broken (Ecclesiastes 4:12). It is not a burden because the person you become involved with acts as a bridge to help carry the burden. When an individual is not carrying their share of the load, it causes the other person to become overwhelmed and unable to find the peace and soul-harmony that should exist in Jesus Christ.

Recognizing and Eliminating Burdens

The question that you should answer is who you should enter into relationship with. Can they make your load easier, or will they make it heavier? If they make your load heavier, they have not been ordained by God to be in your life. Jesus said, "My way is easy."

Let's read it again: "Come to me all of you who work and have heavy loads . . . ." Have you ever had a heavy load? Some of you are married to, friends with, in partnership with, employ, or are employed by a heavy load. Their first name is Heavy, and their last name is Load. Jesus says, "I will give you rest. Follow my teachings and learn from me . . . ."

The reason we are studying this subject is to learn how relationships are designed to work; instinctively we do not know. That is why the divorce rate in this country is over 50 percent. Half of all marriages make it, half do not. One reason has to do with where couples place their focus. Some people spend large amounts of money on weddings—money they do not have, money they borrowed, money they need to live off of after they are married—and they do not remain married two years. Someone needs to teach how relationships should operate. All the days may not be good days, but there is supposed to be a person who is helping you shoulder the load. I am not saying every day you'll be laughing, "Ha ha ha, hee hee hee." You are not going to jump over the moon all of the time my brother, my sister, but the individual who is in your life is supposed to be there to help you carry the load, not increase the load capacity.

If you are thinking of getting into a relationship with someone, you can refer to this book to determine whether it is of God or not. If they are making your way hard, it is not of God. This is so simple, but how many of you will go out and do it? Some of you will read this book and return to the heavy load Satan placed in your life, because you "love them" or "need them." People will wear out their pastor or advisor trying to get him or her to fix that person, but there is only one thing you can do about a heavy load who refuses to change. That is why they make dump trucks.

I would not allow someone to put a heavy load on me, neither should anyone else. Jesus says to bring it to Him. You do not have to carry some things. If it is making you heavy, it is not of God. If you are crying more nights than you are peaceful, it is not of God.

I use this principle in my personal life. I also use it for selecting leaders in the church. If they make my way hard, I make the necessary adjustments to replace them. They are not supposed to be here to bring difficulty into my life; they should be here to help me carry the load. I even use this same principle to determine who is going to be my friend. I am not teaching you something I do not live by. If they are making my way hard, I stop dealing with them.

I even know some ministers who are heavy loads. I love them and I can receive from them, but sometimes they make things hard. Do you know what I do? I stay away from them. I feed them with a long-handled spoon. They may mean well, but if they are making my life too complicated, it is not worth it; life is difficult enough by virtue of the fact that it is life. It is not wise to reach out and take something into your life that will make it more difficult, more challenging.

Think about this. A lot of women are attracted to men because of the appealing way they look. Looks might not make your load lighter, honey. As a matter of fact, those looks may be high maintenance. I know some women who do not like handsome men because it is perceived that their maintenance is too high. They tell me, "It's too hard to keep a good-looking man. Give me the man who's kind of unattractive." These women are drawn to men who look like a hidden mystery, sort of an enigma, a shrouded mystery, kind of underneath the rock. They recognize there is something good inside of them, but when anyone else looks at them, they can't see it. These women, however, declare, "That is the one I want!" Some beautiful women are like this as well. For them, the opposite gender's upkeep is hard to maintain because the competition is so great. It is not wise to base your attraction to a person or reason for entering into an association on appearances alone.

This is generally speaking, however. It is not an absolute, praise the Lord. Every man likes something good to look at. Some women say, "My husband likes me plain." Okay, watch who he looks at when he is not looking in your direction. He is not looking at a woman who doesn't have her hair groomed, I promise you! Some argue, "He just likes me when I'm nappy-headed and ashy." No, he does not, he just told you that. Your husband does not like your appearance because when it comes to women on the street, he is not looking at the nappy-headed ones. He's looking at someone who has a little somethin' somethin' going on!

Let me share another thing the Lord told me. He said, "Sometimes the individual who is directly involved in a particular relationship is benefitted, but the rest of those concerned are tormented. That is still a burden." In other words, if you are in a relationship with a person and you're telling everyone, "He's all right with me," but your mother, father, sister, brother, and everyone else is being tormented by that person, the Lord said that it is still a burden. If this is the case, it may be that your eyes are blind, and then it is only a matter of time before they will be opened. Then you will see that the relationship is a burden. Think about it, beloved. If everyone in your circle of significant persons is being tormented and you are the only one who is being benefitted, can that really be a blessing? A blessing from God will be a blessing overall.

A person's own mother may be telling you, "Honey, you better know what you're doing." When someone's mother talks to you like this, listen to her; because a mother is supposed to love her son almost more than she loves her own life. If she tells you something like this, you had better close your head to all the charm being put on you and listen.

When God gives people to each other, whether it is ministry, business, friendly, passionate, or marital relationship, it is an overall blessing. Let's examine this by percentages. There may be one or two persons in your circle who disapprove of your significant other person, but the greater percentage should be blessed by that person. If the individual comes into your family or alliances and sets them at odds, you have a stinker. It matters not what he or she looks like nor the educational level of that person, you have a bomb. A bridge will be a bridge, if not for everyone, for most. You will be able to tell if God has placed this relationship in your life because it will offer bridging capacities to many. You will see them reaching out to help a number of people, not just you. I have seen men who only invest in the woman they desire, but not the rest of the family, not the mother nor anyone else.

How many wives will agree that their husbands acted one way before marriage and changed once they married them? I know I have changed some. I apologized to my wife for not doing the things I used to. Now, my time is just zapped. I have to schedule time to meet with her. I used to run and open doors for her. There were times before we got married when she would come out from her job, and a nicely wrapped gift with bows, flowers, anything from roses to orchids would be on her car. I mean, I was just spending my money. I still do special things now. She can never and will never say I missed any special days.

Brothers, listen to me. If you want to keep your woman happy, calendar special days. Remember Valentine's Day *and* your anniversary date. Yes, it was you at the altar saying "I do." Women are not like men. They get a big charge, a big kick out of celebrating those special days. You have to remember that and never forget it. Also, remember her birthday and act as if she is 10 years younger. Tell her, "You look like you're 20, just like my teenaged bride." And men, do not forget your mothers! My mother can stand by the mailbox waiting because she knows her gift is coming like clockwork.

A Bridge: Your Way Over to the Other Side of Life

A bridge by definition is that which is used to cross a stream or a ravine. It also means that which is used to go across. Have any of you ever felt like you were in a good relationship, but you ended up falling in the water, by yourself, sinking or drowning, while that other person went across and left you in the water? That was a burden, not a bridge. When God places a person in your life, they will help you go over. That applies to any type of relationship.

We must be watchful of a dominating spirit that has come into the earth. The youth are wrestling with this as possessive older people use manipulation in an attempt to control them. Women try to control other young women, and older men attempt to control younger men. That is of the devil, not of God. There are couples who have been only dating for two weeks or so, and the young man demands his girlfriend to notify him when she leaves home. If I became aware of a young man addressing my daughter in this manner, I would call him over to my home and say, "Look, she has a father. We are not allowing you to come around here to be her daddy. In fact, you are not even old enough to be her father." If he is, he will catch the devil from me, yes, Amen!

A Burden: It's Time to Lay it Down

A burden, by definition, is a load or a weight; the assignment of weight; an onerous or difficult concern. While you are contemplating that definition, reflect on people who have brought an excessive load into your life that weighted you down. The Bible says in Hebrews 12:1, "Lay aside every weight and the sin that doth so easily beset us." It continues, "Run with patience the race that is set before us, Looking unto Jesus the author and finisher of our faith."

You cannot progress with speed when you are weighted down. I will say it differently. You cannot win when you are weighted down. Some of you are depressed about someone God released out of your life to set you free, and here you are depressed. They were a weight weighing you down. You were so heavy because of that "joker," or "jokeress," that you could not accomplish what God wanted you to accomplish. God opened that door and got them out. You say the devil took them away. No, God took them away, because you were weighted down. There are some people who add additional responsibilities onto you, more than what you should be carrying.

One type of weight some people are needlessly experiencing is the financial support of their adult children. I am from the "old school" to a certain degree, so when I use the word adult, I am referring to people ages 21 and older. I do not think children are grown at 18; they still are immature. Too many things have not jelled in their minds yet. Legally they may be grown, but in my mind, in my sense of thinking, they are grown at age 21. I feel a certain responsibility for my children and will do things for them until that age. They are in another category thereafter because they bring added responsibility.

Some of you are taking care of your 35-year-old child, as well as a grandchild. Listen to me well. That is an additional responsibility that is not yours. I tell my sons now, "Don't get girls pregnant! Don't do what it takes to get them pregnant, because your 'paw paw' doesn't feel like being a 'grand paw paw.'" Even if I were, I am not a babysitter. Some of you are weighted down, loaded down, and your children are steadily having more children. That's a burden. Some of you, God bless your souls, have 40-year-old children who are still borrowing money from you. You need to kick that habit. They are 40 years old! You should be receiving monetary gifts of appreciation from them. That is a load, a heavy responsibility.

This book emphasizes getting in right relationship with God in order to have right relationships in the earth. If you do not have this, and you are not receiving correct understanding from God—which leads to correct actions so that as you reach adult age you have what you are supposed to—your life will be thrown out of kilter. I am not raising my children to be totally dependent upon me all of their lives. Understand that when you have too many adults in your home, they can destroy your family structure. Remember how you thought you were grown and your parents couldn't tell you anything? "Get out," they said to you. "Get your own house if you think you're fully grown. Get your own house!" Do not bring that added responsibility on yourself; it makes your hair gray prematurely.

An exception to all of this may be children who are serious college students. When your children are in college, you do have a responsibility there. Help them as long as they are productive and working sufficiently toward completion. Even when they are in college and reach ages 26 through 30, they may need to figure out a way to financially supplement their education. Perhaps you should plan to help them with the first four years, maybe even five. (The bachelor's degree doesn't necessarily come in four years anymore.) Be mindful that some children will just play you! If they are taking one class per semester or quarter, they will never get out of school. They can be 45 years old telling you, "I'm in school, mama." You are not wise to go for that. Let the added responsibility go; it is a burden.

David, Jonathan, and Saul
(Jonathan: David's Bridge)

We are going to compare David's relationship with Jonathan, who was a bridge, and with Saul, who was a burden. David and Saul's relationship reminds me of a song by Jesse James entitled "I Can Do Bad By Myself." You can do badly by yourself, but you also can do well by yourself. For example, a young woman can become educated and obtain a good job, then get involved with a deadbeat. He uses her car and does nothing, while she is going to work doing something. That's a burden. She can't even go to lunch when she wants to because he is scooting around all day in her car. I do not understand it. Some women lay on their back-end to have children, and can't even find their men within a year after the child's birth. Some people say, "Pastor, you're too graphic," but I tell them that I have the gift of being graphic. That's one of my gifts, and I do not squelch it because it works for me.

If you are living like this, let me explain what you are doing, my kind sister. You have an intimate encounter with a man for, at best,

30 seconds to one minute of maximum pleasure; now a child is conceived inside you. In that moment of pleasure that only lasted, in the more extreme sense, five to seven minutes, you are left with a child who you have to provide for by yourself for the next 18 to 21 years. Now, do the math. Are the 21 years of bondage worth the 30 seconds to seven minutes of pleasure? Let me tell you something, raising children is not as easy or as much fun as getting children. I know women are going through a difficult ordeal of being chaste. I know where your pressure is, but listen, beloved, just do the math. My father used to say in a funny way, "It don't worth it."

Let's progress with our example of David's relationships. I Samuel 18:1-4 of the Amplified Bible reads, "When David had finished speaking with Saul, the soul of Jonathan was knit with the soul of David, and Jonathan loved him as his own life."

That is when you will know you have a bridge. Whether it be a business, marital, friendly, or dating relationship that should consummate in a marriage, you can always measure one's level of affection by this meter: when they love you like they love themselves. That is when you know a person has been ordained by God to be in your life, as a bridge. When they love you as they love themselves, they won't do anything to you that they would not do to themselves. I have searched myself on this one. The Lord said in Ephesians 5:28 that a man should love his wife as he loves himself, as he loves his own flesh. I'll be honest with you, I am still working on that. I have done some things to people that I would not do to myself, and when the Lord looks at it, He says that is not real love. Just chew on that.

Read Verse 2 in our scriptural reference taken from I Samuel, "Saul took David that day, and would not let him return to his father's house." On the right side of that verse, write the word "burden," and on the right side of Verse 1, write the word "bridge," so every time you pass through this scripture, you will remember what I am referring to. "Then Jonathan made a covenant with David." Write over this phrase "bridge." A person who is ordained by God to be a bridge in your life does not mind making a covenant with you. That is why when you sense a person putting pressure on you to give away your special gift, you should know that this is not the will of God for your life. We used to have a saying in the old church, "No ringee, no thingee." A person who says they love you, will adjust for you.

The Lord once gave me a revelation that I did not ask for. I have shared it with my congregation, and I will share it with you. He revealed to me that there is a difference between a man who rents a house and the one who buys a house. If you are 16 or 17 years old and are sexually active, you are being rented. The renter will bump into the structure of the house, pull the coverings off the wall, and break out windows. No amount of care is involved because someone else owns the house. Someone else has to bear responsibility for its maintenance. However, when the same person buys a house, he or she will say, "Get off the grass! Don't you see the grass I've planted?" It's really all dirt, but it now has to be protected, you see. If a person loves you, that person will make a covenant with you. If the person is not willing to make a covenant with you to protect you and your concerns, to be there for you, to be a bridge for you, the person does not love you. That person only loves what you have, or what you can provide, and not who you are.

There is a difference between someone loving your sexual reproductive organ and loving you. There are some people who will lie with you at night, yet, they will not be seen with you during the day. They love the organ, but they do not love the person. There are some people who will lay up with you and won't even talk with you the next day. They will not greet you in public, speak to you, go anywhere with you, forget it! I will address this to women because this is one of their fallacies. Many women think that because men react to the female organ, they are responding to them.

Love will cause a person to strip themselves of what they have to provide for the person they are in a relationship with. In I Samuel 18:4, Jonathan stripped himself for David. Men, right or wrong, when a woman loves you, sometimes she will even strip herself of her own beliefs to get you, to be with you. The comparison is true for a man, whether it's wrong or right. When a man strips himself for a woman, he cares about her. When you are willing to strip yourself, you care to some degree. If you are involved with someone who is never willing to strip some area for you or make the appropriate adjustments, the person does not love you, and that person eventually will become a burden.

CHAPTER 2

Benefits of Godly Relationships

Godly Relationships Produce Peace

As I stated in the previous chapter, most of what I am teaching regarding relationships is best explained in percentages. No one person will bring a harmonious flow into your life 100 percent of the time, simply because he or she is a human being. Your relationship will have a degree of disharmony at various points, but largely that individual should bring peace. Your God-ordained "other" should be easy to get along with.

Initially, however, this may not appear to be the case. Men and women are so different that it may take a while for peace to evolve. It may take time and patience for a couple to learn, deal with, and cope with each other's personalities in order to reach a level of harmony.

Before I was married, I thought I was the best man in the world, but shortly thereafter, I had a change of mind. I began to think I was the worst man in the world because my wife cried a lot, sometimes all of the time. We would be fine during breakfast, but after we had eaten, I would lose her. Whenever I walked through the house and saw the bathroom door closed, I grew to know not to pass the bathroom because the few times I did, she was in there sobbing. I would ask her, "What's wrong?" "Nothing," she would say. "What did I do to you?" "Nothing," she'd repeat. "Do you need me to do something for you?" "Uh, uh." "Are you hurting?" "I just feel sad," she'd finally say.

Now as a man, I was lost. I didn't know how to deal with a woman's emotional responses, because everything I deal with as a man is either one way or the other. Men are very logistical beings; we only understand "A" or "B." We do not understand when it is A and a half of something else. We are lost! So we need God in our fellowships in order to understand each other. This is true in marriage as it is in other partnerships.

One of the greatest revelations I have received in marriage is the fact that my wife is not supposed to be exactly like me nor are any persons who are in any relationship. Their association is in place so that their opposites enhance each other's weaknesses. Biologically, we are structured differently, but I assumed my job was to help her become like me in other areas. I was working hard at it, too. I thought I was supposed to correct all her imperfections, as if I had none. I just couldn't see my own because I was too busy working on hers. Finally, the Lord told me He made us both differently. I had to learn how to appreciate the differences and allow them to affect me in a positive way, and allow my differences to affect her in a positive way.

You might say, "Okay, I have a child who is something of a burden to me. What do I do? I can't divorce my child." If your child is an adult, you may have to mentally divorce him or her with distance or space. You may have to separate yourself from the anguish of your child's welfare after your child reaches a certain age. Some parents worry about their children to such a degree that their distress puts a strain on the relationship. Instead of a bridge, it becomes a burden.

We as believers must turn some matters over to the Lord and let Him work them out. We cannot wrestle with them and keep their heaviness on our minds. The struggle will wear us out. It will cause us to be physically, mentally, and spiritually exhausted. It will not wear Jesus out. He tells us to cast our care upon Him. Why? He cares for us (I Peter 5:7). In other words, He is going to handle your problems for you. Some of you may even be concerned with loved ones, family members or associates who are sick, dying, incarcerated, addicted to chemical substances, or facing other kinds of challenges. Roll that concern over on the Lord; God doesn't want you worried about it. Ultimately, He wants to give you rest for your mind (soul).

A Godly Relationship Will Bring Increase

If you are going to be married (whether in the literal or figurative manner), and that is what Godly dating, interviewing, or pacing should qualify one for, you need someone to help multiply and add pleasures in your life, instead of dividing and subtracting accomplishments away. Some women, for instance, have trouble getting this right. They say, "The Lord sent him, but he just doesn't have a good job yet." Well, if the Lord sent him, let the Lord work on him until He elevates his lifestyle, at least to where you are. This way, both of you can bring your fortunes together, even small fortunes, and have a bridge.

If, for example, he is earning $7,000 annually, he cannot adequately take care of himself with that income. If you are earning $20,000 annually, which barely takes care of you and your car payment, how can you believe the Lord sent you "a blessing?" If you choose to marry such a fellow, in a few days after the "honey" slips off the "moon," how blessed do you really believe you will feel? Many people are so eager to marry (into situations) that they are blinded by the fantasy or expectation of what that marriage will produce. They rush into the relationship with unrealistic expectations, instead of counting the cost it will take to support one another. His $7,000 will not help you much financially. When the two of you bring your bills together and sit down to look at them, you will find that his income is taking away from you. You may discover that he's not the wrong man, but that he may just need time to improve himself. By the way, you should address this issue before the marriage ceremony or any contract is enforced.

Agape Love: A Key Ingredient in Godly Relationships

Let's return to I Samuel 18:1 of the Amplified version. From Verse 1 to Verse 4, write the word "burden" over the name Saul, and over the name Jonathan, write the word "bridge."

"So when David had finished speaking, the soul of Jonathan (the bridge) was knit to the soul of David, and Jonathan (the bridge) loved him as his own life."

As I already have stated, if God has placed you in a relationship with someone, or some business status, there will be agape love. That person will love you unconditionally. There are people in the body of Christ who tell their partners they love them, but if their partner upsets them, that "love" is challenged. I tell people all the time not to marry or enter into any relationship with anyone until you see them upset. This is a revelation for many because the last thing we want to see is our significant other person or business others upset, especially on our way to the altar of decision. It is important to consider this issue beforehand, because when you decide to marry or engage in relationship, you enter into a lifelong commitment. You decide to accept your partner's problems for life. So, while you're in the dating stage, see how your partner responds to the feeling of being upset.

One thing my wife has learned about me that she didn't know before we were married is that when I'm upset because of a senseless thing I've done, I scold myself. I "go off." I do not curse. I do not kick the dog or strangle the goldfish out of the aquarium or anything like that. I go off on myself. I just hate to do something stupid.

Once she asked me to paint a wall inside the house in which we were living. It was a quarter wall, off the entrance foyer. We had mauve carpet and she wanted a subtle iridescent effect on the wall. It was white, but she wanted me to paint it a light, contrasting color. So I went to the store, bought an expensive paint, and completed the task. She commented, "Oh, you're doing a good job." And I was doing fine, until I began to touch up a little area. I had to shake the paint to get it all mixed up together, but I didn't check the lid because I thought I put it on tight. I began shaking the container of paint, and it splattered everywhere. The wallpaper and the new floor covering in the kitchen both were damaged. She was standing there looking at me, smiling. I slammed the can down, and boy, was I angry. I said, "That's just so stupid, that's stupid! I can't believe I did something stupid like that!" She said, "George you're human." I told her, "But it's stupid! I don't do stupid things like that! Oh, I hate doing stupid things!" I went on for about 10 or 15 minutes. I was upset with myself because I hate doing senseless things. It drives me up the wall!

My wife then received a revelation of how her husband acts when he does something embarrassing. She knows now to get out of the way because I can be upset for a while. Some of you need to apply that principle to people you are in relationships with. Let them air themselves. See how they act in a moment of anger. You may find they are prone to do things you thought they otherwise would not do. You can discover this before saying, "I do," "you're hired," or any other note of commitment.

We must understand that a person's upbringing plays a vital role in the person's behavioral patterns. Some men and women were raised in abusive, dysfunctional households and respond to anger in the same manner they saw their parents respond. You might not have known their background before becoming involved with them. Perhaps that was one of the interview questions you forgot to ask before saying "I do," and now you are startled at their conduct. They get upset and jump on people, curse, and slam cabinet doors, and you sit there thinking, "Wwhha! Wwhha!" He, or she, is upper cutting, jabbing, and kicking you, and you can't even relate to what is going on. Always allow them to get upset before the relationship is a committed one.

In relationships, the No. 1 component that should be present is "agape" love. Jonathan loved David as his own life. Ephesians 5:28 says, "Husbands ought to love their wives as their own flesh." It is serious to talk about loving someone like you love yourself. That means you are willing to do for another person everything you are willing to do for yourself. That means if you cannot do it for your spouse, then you cannot do it for yourself. Men, if you cannot buy your wife a new suit, then you should not buy one for yourself. That is where you are headed with your marital relationship. You will invest a lot into your partner, so be sure you have a high level of attraction for them. Let me share a bit of advice with you. If you do not like your mate before you are married, do not get married. Affection generally does not go up, it goes down in the valley and spins around in the commode for a while! Maybe if you get in the Word, it will go up to the mountain after a while.

People do not want to hear this before marriage. They do not believe it. They are only concerned with the sexual part. "Baby, it's going to be on! I've been waiting for this a long time!" Unfortunately, some people already have explored that aspect of marriage during courtship. You may have gotten ahead of God's perfect plan without realizing there are people who only are interested in your sexual organ, or the way you operate your sexual organ. They may not be attracted to you as a person. You think, "I have them wrapped around my finger." Your reproductive organ may have them wrapped around your finger, but there is a difference between it and you. That is what happens in some cases when people presume love brought them into relationships. It was not love for the person, it was the love of lust. That type of love does not last. It is the thought of what will be received rather than what will be given.

As a marriage progresses, sexual intercourse, as gratifying as it can be, becomes a very small part of the relationship. It is not a big thing. After a while you realize, "Hey, this is the person I sleep with every single night." Your mate is like a pastor in that your mate is with you all of the time. You see, the evangelist comes and preaches for a while and leaves, but people expect the pastor to keep coming up with something new.

Men, for example, are fascinated with women because of what we can't see or can't touch. We are curious about what we don't know and don't see. This keeps the chase on. For example, the index finger is a part of the body that is constantly exposed, so people are not intrigued by it. The main difference between the index finger and a woman's breasts is the fact that her breasts are usually covered from plain view. A man will not see a woman's finger and say, "That's a *pretty* finger." He isn't going to wait at a woman's house all night just to see her finger. However, he might miss out on anything just to see that which is covered. Why? It is covered. It's a body part just like other body parts, but because it is covered, there is intrigue. Once a person's best gift is uncovered, it becomes just like the finger. If one sees it over and over again like seeing the finger, it becomes just as common. No one told you this prior to the relationship.

Once you have married someone, you frequently see them in their barest form. They get dressed in front of you while you casually are lying around. They may even go to sleep undressed. Because of your familiarity with them, the drive you otherwise would experience is minimized. For this reason, married couples should watch how they go to sleep. Take extra measures to prepare yourself before going to bed. It is important that your spouse finds you physically desirable, even at bedtime. There are some wives who still sleep in long flannel pajamas with feet in them. All they need is a set of long, floppy ears on their heads and they will look like Bugs Bunny rather than a desirable mate.

That's the way a marriage is. The covers are pulled off and all of the intrigue and mystery are gone. Now it's just you. Bad breath in the morning. Occasional hair rollers at night. You see it just like it is. The question is, do you love the person or do you just love the way they look or do you love what they have?

Time Will Reveal if You are Connected with a Bridge or a Burden

In I Samuel 18:2, "Saul, (the burden) took David that day and would not let him return to his father's house." A burden will appear to be a blessing initially, but give it some time and you will discover what they really are. Soon they will come from behind the facade they used to attract you. I have counseled many people who've said, "They were fine before we got married . . . ." I tell them, "No they weren't, you were just in love. You were blind and 'outta' your mind." They were so in love with that person that they could not see the person's faults. They weren't in the right frame of mind to look at the person's actions before entering into the relationship, to determine if he or she would be a bridge or burden.

You see, people really don't change a lot from their original dispositions. Salvation will change their spirit, but as far as the soul and relationships are concerned, people must be willing to renew their minds in order to change. They were the way they are now, you just didn't wait long enough to find this out. Saul was a burden from the beginning, and God knew it. He did not want Saul to be king, but the people insisted and He granted their request (I Samuel 8:1-22). God even told Samuel that even though the people wanted Saul, he would never work, he was a burden.

God has told some of you a particular person will never benefit you. Are you so consumed by the things the person does for you that you fail to see the larger picture? "Look what they bought me!" They bought you a ring; they gave gifts—okay. Have you sold yourself out for a ring? A bracelet? The devil has plenty of gold he will give to you if it means you will sell yourself out and miss God's best. When that person has walked out of your life, that ring and bracelet will be meaningless because you will have lost a vital part of yourself.

Bridges are People of Covenant

Let's return to I Samuel 18:3, "Then Jonathan and David made a covenant, because he loved him as his own soul." The bridge always makes a covenant, not a promise; a covenant, not a wish.

I have discovered that some women, perhaps all, love conversation. Some love it to such a degree that they will commit to a man who is unwilling to make a covenant with them simply because he's a smooth talker. He knows what to say and tells them exactly what they want to hear. I told a man one day, "You don't need to have any money in this day and time. You don't have to have a good job. You don't even have to look all that good. Just be neat and keep yourself up a little bit. Keep your body a little fit and trim. Have command over the English language. And, you can have all the women your Rolodex can stand."

Women love for men to talk to them. A man can say, "Hey baby, you look so nice," and she will talk to him all day. Women also will make themselves look nice and walk around a man just to see if he is going to tell them they look good. Their mind-set is, "Say it again. I ain't heard it in a while, say it again!" Women love talk, but God says relationships cannot be comprised of talk alone. They must include covenant. What is he willing to do? What is she willing to do? What is your associate or partner willing to give up for you?

In relationships, people use all sorts of rationales to persuade their partners to "prove" their love for them. Some say, "If you love me, you'll sleep with me." In order to determine if someone who is pressuring you to sleep with them loves you, use this litmus test: tell him or her to make a covenant. Tell the person to wait until you marry them. Most will show you a ghost. They will leave quickly. If the person loves your whole package, all of you, not just the sexual part, he or she will wait for marriage. Jesus told a parable about a man finding a pearl in a field. Because of his find, he will go home and sell everything. He will put a "For Sale" sign on his home, if necessary, or have a garage sale. He will sell everything he has to try to get enough money to buy the whole field because he found one pearl in it (St. Matthew 13:45-46). Honey, if someone tells you they love you and desire you, tell the person to make a covenant. Tell them to wait for you, to marry you. If he really loves you, he will work like a slave. You'll call him Mandingo, Toby, Chicken George, or a name similar to one of these because he will work like a slave to marry you.

Take a look at Jacob, for example. His father-in-law, Laban, had a daughter named Rachel for whom he worked seven years to marry. Not only did Jacob not marry Rachel at the end of the time period as Laban promised, but he was tricked into marrying her sister, Leah, instead. He worked an additional seven years to marry the woman he truly desired. Laban knew what he had. He knew Rachel was very beautiful. He probably thought, "I'm saving her for a man who will be so in love with her that I can trick him and pawn off Leah, my other daughter."

Leah's name meant "lazy-eyed." She had a condition that caused her eyes to cross, and she probably wasn't very attractive. Leah did not have all of the superlatives going for her, and Laban decided to find someone to marry her because she was a burden to him (Genesis 29). Now here comes Jacob. He went to water the cattle one day and saw Rachel. He said, "Good God! That's a fine woman."

Men always are impressed by their sense of sight and smell. This is why I advise women to always look and smell good, praise the Lord. One time a man said to me, "I always wanted to know what it felt like to love a woman so much that you would do anything for her." He continued, "I never felt it, until I met this woman." He was so taken by her appearance that he left his wife, family, and financial stability to pursue her.

Now, Jacob prepares for Rachel. Jacob is a man of wealth and influence, so he feels he stands a good chance of persuading Laban to allow him to marry Rachel. He goes to her father and says, "Laban, I gotta have your daughter." "No problem. You want her?," Laban asks. Jacob answers, "Yeah." Laban says, "Come, be my slave for seven years, then you can have her." Jacob had only kissed her once, and he was impressed with the way she carried herself. Have you ever been around a woman or a man who has the kind of godly confidence, that when you come into his or her presence, there is something about the chemistry between both of you that you cannot shake? This is what Jacob experienced.

He worked for Rachel seven years as an indentured servant! At the end of those years Jacob says, "Look, whew! I've been sweating, and not only because I've been working in the fields either." He said, "Man, I've been looking at that woman for seven years. Laban, I served my time. Give her to me! I've got to have her. I can't wait another day." Laban says, "All right. I'm throwing a party for your pre-wedding celebration. Get some wine and party things. I'll have some other women there. Just talk and fraternize with the guests, and I'll have a female servant prepare Rachel for you. And after the midnight ceremony you can have her."

Using my spiritual imagination, I can see the night is pitch black. After the night wedding, Jacob was in the tent thinking he was copulating with Rachel. He did not find out until the next day that his wife was Leah instead. Unfortunately, he realized he married the wrong woman after sleeping with her, having consummated the marriage and taken responsibility for her for the rest of his life, according to Hebrew tradition.

Do you know what he does? He goes right back to Laban and says, "Hey that was a fast one. If I had a daughter that looked like Leah, I would have done the same thing." He says, "What will it take for me to get Rachel because I still want her." Laban tells him, "Man, give me seven more years." Jacob went right back to work for seven additional years. At the end of that period, Jacob finally married Rachel.

Even Leah knew that Jacob loved Rachel more than he loved her. What I'm trying to tell you, beloved, is when a man or a woman really loves you, they will give themselves for you. They will work for you. They will wait for you. They will honor you. They'll come back and tell you when they were wrong about something. They may even break up with you, but they'll come back.

A Bridge Gives

Another way to determine if you have a bridge in your life is to examine their giving patterns. Are you receiving anything from them? If so, what and how much do you actually receive? Do they give their best? Bridges virtually have no limit to what they'll give to those they are in relationship with, and as this next scripture shows, they will give completely of themselves in spite of their own need.

"And Jonathan stripped himself of the robe that was upon him, and gave it to David, and his garments, even to his sword, and to his bow, and to his girdle" (I Samuel 18:4).

When God has ordained a person to become involved with you, they will take what is theirs and give it to you. They will not take what is yours to use it for themselves. I remember when my wife and I were first married, she used to tell me all the time, "You know, love always gives." I used to hate it when she would tell me that because I knew what was coming next. She was going to tell me right then that she was always giving in to me, and it was true. I was selfish and didn't even know it. That is why I advise men when I counsel that if they are selfish, we will either end the meeting or discuss how they are going to rid themselves of selfishness. There are two things that will tear down any relationship: selfishness and jealousy.

If you are a jealous person, begin giving more of yourself. This is true, especially for men, because God has ordained men to be His authority or representation in the earth. The scope of that authority is measured by man's ability to love. You do not have to knock a woman in the head to get her to follow you, just love her. She will follow you anywhere you go if you love her. There is another thing I've found about women. They generally will not resist a giving man. Some of you sisters said you were going to leave your man, but he gave to you the gift of love, and you hung right on in there.

It is the same way with a church, place of employment, or business. No one has to knock people over the head to get followers or customers, just love them. Members will come right into your church. Some people try to be authority figures with force; however, authority is measured out by the ability to love.

Women are counting on men for love. Many women are without the love of a man, and without his headship, they can be out of balance. In some cases, because of their emotional nature, they do not have a consistent picture of themselves. A woman may think she looks good today, but tomorrow she will think she looks bad, and the devil will send someone with sweet talk the very same day she is feeling unattractive. If a woman does not have a man in her life, she should find a good church with a pastor who is strong in leadership. A pastor who is willing to give godly love and direction will help her remain balanced.

A Bridge Behaves Wisely

If you have ever been in a relationship with a person who behaved in such a highly inappropriate manner that you became embarrassed or frustrated, then you can appreciate the value of having someone who knows how to conduct themselves.

I Samuel 18:5 says, "And David went out whithersoever Saul sent him, and behaved himself wisely: and Saul set him over the men of war . . . ." He went wherever the burden sent him and he prospered. When you are a God-given person who is ready for a relationship, you will know how to behave yourself.

I have talked to people who say they don't have any friends, and I tell them to examine their ways. Behave yourself wisely and you will prosper. Be loveable. You may say, "I want more friends, I want a man." If you are a mean woman, no man is coming into your life to stay. As quickly as he discovers how mean you are, he'll leave. The same thing applies to men. A woman will not be around to stay if you are mean. Some people may say, "Well, I don't see how Mrs. Matthews can tolerate him. He just seems like he's too focused." But you see, I don't bark all of the time. I know how to meow, meow, meow! When I go home, I take my suit and my tie off; I take my preacher off, and I am a man.

My wife was raised to be real "holy" and "saved," and I told her when we were first married, "We don't need any church field missionaries in this bedroom. Don't come in here trying to preach Bible verses, scriptures, or sing with praise tapes, not when we are getting ready to be romantically involved. I just want you to be a tigress!"

A lady once told us, "I just know your house must be the most anointed place in the world because your wife is so anointed and you are so anointed." I said to the woman, "Thank you for the compliment, but underneath it all I am a man and she is a woman." She wears nice soft things, and she doesn't wear a choir robe to bed, and neither do I.

A bridge will know the appropriate manner to conduct themselves in every situation that comes. Whether in our friendships, marriages, sibling relationships, or any other kind of relationship, the Spirit of God can teach your bridge how to behave wisely.

A Bridge Communicates

Healthy relationships thrive when both partners enjoy open communication. A couple should be able to express their concerns, thoughts, and feelings with one another and receive adequate feedback to let them know their partner has an interest in what they have shared. Let's use the example of Jonathan and David to see what the Bible says regarding communication in relationships. I Samuel 20:1 reads, "And David fled from Naioth in Ramah, and came and said before Jonathan (the bridge), 'What have I done? What is mine iniquity? And what is my sin before thy father (the burden), that he seeketh my life?'"

You always can go to the bridge and find out where trouble is, because a bridge gives answers. All of the persons God has truly placed in your life will talk to you. I hate being in a restaurant with people who visibly have a problem with something that occurred, but when asked if anything is wrong, they won't tell. I cannot figure out what it is, and they will not communicate with me. A bridge will talk to you. Why? Because he or she will help you cross over, and you cannot cross over without communication.

When a man is in a relationship with a woman, he wants to know how she feels about what he does. "You know baby, tell me, is this cologne too strong?" "Do you like what I'm wearing?" "Tell me, what is it about me you don't like? Is it my charisma? Tell me, I'll change it, but you have to tell me something."

Even ask your friends if you offend them. In any kind of relationship, be it friendly, parental, or so forth, let those you are involved with tell you how they feel about you. I talk to my parents and if they upset me or if we do not see eye-to-eye on something, we talk about it. A bridge is always communicating.

A Bridge Will Promote Your Life

In I Samuel 20:2, Jonathan answers the questions David posed in the preceding section. "And he said unto him, 'God forbid; thou shalt not die . . . .'" The bridge is always giving life.

If God places a person in your life for a good relationship, they will always promote your life, your longevity. If you are married, contemplating marriage, or desire being married at some point in your life, I'd like to clear up a misconception. The Word of God says, ". . . They twain shall become one flesh" (Genesis 2:24). The "one flesh" statement indicates that the putting together of the male responsibilities with the female responsibilities in marriage becomes one entity. However, while the couple is one flesh, the individuals involved still have two separate personalities. Do not try to make your spouse just like you. Your mate may not have the same interests you have. He or she may want to continue their education and you may not. You do not have to be on the same page as it relates to a situation such as this one.

Some people think that because they are in a relationship, they have to go everywhere with their significant other. That is not the case. To promote your life, a bridge will give you certain amounts of space. Doing so will cause you to grow and develop other areas of your life. In other words, it will cause your life to be, overall, promoted.

CHAPTER 3

Producing Relationships of Harmony

===

I was speaking with the Lord one day, and He made me realize that much information needs to be given as it relates to relationships. We need to be inundated with godly teaching to such a degree that we take on the mind of Christ concerning relationships. We need His influence because we largely do not know how to coexist with each other. This is almost a primitive thought, but it is true. All you have to do is look at television or read a newspaper, and you will conclude the same.

There are some in the same Christian faith and fellowship who do not get along harmoniously because of jealousy. A single woman cannot sit by another woman's husband in church assemblies because the married woman thinks the single woman desires him for herself. (Some single women, however, may want the husband.) With some married women, it is an even stroke; they want to change partners with someone whom they are not in relationship. As you can see, we need a lot of teaching on relationships.

As time progresses, many things enter into the body of Christ regarding this topic, and pastors have to teach people what the Word of God has to say. It is a broad subject. Largely, men do not know how to get along with women, and in many cases, women definitely do not know how to get along with other women. Just stating the natural facts, 9 times out of 10, men can get along with each other. They won't have a lot of trouble in one-on-one relationships, unless one is effeminate. For these reasons, I am dealing with relationships and offering solutions to many of the problems people encounter.

We discussed earlier that God places a person in your life to help ease your load, and the relationship should be a bridge that enables you to cross over to the other side of your situations. We also learned that a burden is a load or a weight; any oppressive responsibility. I shared with you that if your relationship is not God-ordained, it is probably of the enemy, Satan, and it is a burden.

Recall the illustration of percentages. Let's say that 60 to 80 percent of the time the person in question is a bridge, and maybe 10 to 20 percent of the time they are a burden.

This is normal. If these statistics are inverted and they are a bridge only 10 to 20 percent of the time and a burden 60 to 80 percent, something is wrong with the relationship. If they are heavier than they are lighter, something is wrong. If you are carrying them more than they are walking with you, something is wrong.

You also will need to factor in the element of time. Give them a little time to straighten the areas in their life that are not quite intact. I often tell people not to marry broken pieces. If you know a car only has three tires, do not try to drive it out of the parking lot. Let it stay there until the dealer puts another tire on it. Some people knowingly marry individuals who are broken. Two people broken into many fragments never come together to make a complete unit.

So what are we looking for in relationships? A bridge. To determine the attributes and characteristics of a bridge and a burden, we will continue looking at scriptures.

A Burden Uses the Bridge

In I Samuel 16:14, Saul is a picture of a burdensome person who has the tendency to take advantage of the person who is the bridge. In the African-American community, we have used the word "usury." We have used a variation of the word in the phrase, "You used me." Have you ever been used? Is someone using you now?

Have you ever used anyone? A burden tends to prey upon its victim in the area of usury. I am telling you that God did not put you in an unequally yoked relationship, because the inequity will make a demand on the individual who does not have the necessary things to offer. The only thing a burden can do is subtract from you. For this reason, women, if a man does not have money and you do, look over him or through him until he does.

Suppose you have been tithing and giving offerings, and the Lord has blessed you by putting you on an even plane financially. Then, some poor person approaches you saying the Lord sent them to you. They must be out of their mind! You should look at them and say, "Not the God I serve." What can this poor person do for you? Nothing but drain your money. You may be thinking, "Well, the Lord is working on them and they are a blessing." Okay, let me tell you what is going to happen when the "blessing" has ended. There's a good chance you and that person will have a conflict over the lack of money, and you are going to be dissatisfied and unhappy. It does not matter how good they look, how fine they are, or how adequate their speech is and how their words make you feel. When the superficial attraction has faded, you will complain about the lack of money. The lack of money will make you fight. You can be in "luv," not love, but not have money, and it will elevate and amplify your disagreements.

Some people cannot get past how good someone looks. Forget that! If they do not have any money, good looks are not going to mean anything after a while. All men ought to strive to have money, so if they happen to meet a woman who strikes their fancy, they'll be able to get along. Men will spend money to date a woman they're serious about. Women, you just have to look good or strike us in that manner, and we'll pay.

Equally Yoked Relationships Bring Balance to Your Life

In relationships, there ought to be equities. You have to look for a balance. Look for people who lend balance to your life, who represent a balance to you. If you are an older person, you ought to look for someone who is just about as old as you are. Now, "old" is a relative term. Old to one person is not necessarily old to someone else. You are looking for balance in your life. If you are young, you should be looking for someone who is young. Unless they have a substantial amount of money and they are old, then you just cross on over, praise the Lord.

I once told my wife, "God forbid that something ever happens to you, but, er, uh . . . ." I continued, "If something were to ever happen, I'm going to have to get a woman younger than you." I added, "She's probably not even born yet." She responded, "And you're out of your mind, because I know you. You won't last." I said, "Who, me? I'm a super preacher." She told me, "No, you aren't. These young girls will burn your mind out. You'll be out preaching for the Lord, and they'll be out at the nightclub. When you come back in from church, your new wife will be gone and won't return until two or three o'clock in the morning, and dare you to ask her why."

After my wife finished testifying to me, I realized if that were to happen, I would need to seek for some equity in age, maturity, and status. I should find someone in my own category. I believe, should that happen, I can live with just me and Jesus. Hallelujah! You probably only need one good marriage in a lifetime anyway. If something ever happened and you see me then, I might have a different mind-set. You know, as you grow, you change.

Burdens Open the Doors to Trouble

There are a lot of things that come into our lives that God did not put on us, and some things the devil did not put on us either. We open the door to some things ourselves. As we will see in I Samuel 16:14, Saul is a prime example of this behavior. "But the Spirit of the Lord departed from Saul, and an evil spirit from the Lord troubled him."

We must rightly divide the Word here to understand that God did not send an evil spirit to come on Saul and torment him. Saul was disobedient, and his actions opened the door for the evil spirit to come in and on him. The Bible says in James 1:13 that, "God cannot be tempted with evil, neither tempteth he any man." James 1:17 tells us, "Every good and perfect gift is from above, and cometh down from the Father of lights, with whom is no variableness, neither shadow of turning."

Now we know that good gifts come from God, and if there was any tormenting activity coming from the adversary at all, it was because Saul opened the door to it. Just like Saul, many of us face trouble because of our own actions. For example, if the temperature is 20 degrees and I go outside in shorts and a T-shirt, I've just opened the door to chances of a cold. God did not have anything to do with that and neither did Satan. I did it to myself.

So too, it is in relationships that some people do negative things to themselves. I have stated earlier that relationships are an option, especially marriage. Everyone does not have to be married. The fact is, no one has to be married. It is *not* mandatory. If you married a person and received a lemon in the deal, you made that decision. God did not force you to do it, and Satan did not twist your arm behind your back. You entered into the relationship of your own free accord; therefore, you should not blame anyone else for what has happened. You made the choice. You were happy when you said "I do." You were happy on your wedding night, so why are you upset now? You went grocery shopping and bought the wrong groceries. You should have purchased a meal, but you got sugar instead. I'll stop there.

I Samuel 16:15-16 reads,

> "And Saul's servant said unto him, 'Behold now, an evil spirit from God troubleth thee. Let our lord command thy servants, which are before thee, to seek out a man, who is a cunning player on an harp: and it shall come to pass, when the evil spirit from God is upon thee, that he shall play with his hand, and thou shall be well'" (The King James Bible).

Now, let's read the remainder of the chapter in The Amplified Bible:

> Verses 17-23 read, "Saul said to his servants, 'Find me a man who plays well, and bring him to me.' One of the young men said, 'I have seen a son of Jesse the Bethlehemite, who plays skillfully; a valiant man, a man of war, prudent in speech, and eloquent, an attractive

person, and the Lord is with him.' So Saul sent messengers and said, 'Send me David, your son who is with sheep.' And Jesse took a donkey, loaded it with bread, a skin of wine, a kid, and sent them by David, his son, to Saul. And David came to Saul and served him." Saul became very fond of him, and he became his armor bearer. Saul sent to Jesse saying, 'Let David remain in my services, for he pleases me.' And when the evil spirit from God was upon Saul, David took a harp and played it. So Saul was refreshed and became well, and the evil spirit left him."

Envision that for a moment. Saul already has gotten into disobedience with God, and the trouble is just beginning. God has withdrawn His spirit from Saul and released His spirit upon a young man named David. Saul is in trouble. He is vexed and tormented by the devil. This is what happens to a lot of people and they begin to look for someone to get them out of torment. Let me tell you something, beloved, peace does not come from people, it comes from God. If you already are in trouble, do not take on a relationship with a person thinking it will break the yoke of troublesomeness. Peace comes from God. Don't ever get into relationship with people looking for peace. Some people go from one bad relationship to another. What are they looking for? They are looking for peace, but it does not come from **man**, it comes from **God**. This same principle applies to personal and business relationships.

I can imagine a conversation between Saul and his servant. Saul's servant says, "Well king, we understand you're in trouble. Actually, you tend to go out of your mind a little bit when this spirit from the enemy comes upon you. Let us find someone who has an anointing from God so they can play. And when they play, that spirit will go from you and you'll be like your normal self." The kings says, "That sounds like a good idea to me. Search the kingdom." One of his servants says, "Oh, we've heard about this young fellow God is just beginning to use out there in the sheepfold. His name is David; he's Jesse's son, his eighth son." Saul says, "Well, send for him." So they go to Jesse's house. When they arrive, Jesse is so impressed the king actually wants one of his sons to come in the castle and minister to him that he sends a gift with the boy. That's what the scripture, "A man's gift makes room for him, and brings him before great men" (Proverbs 18:16) means.

Some people think the gift in this passage of scripture refers to one's special talent or ability that comes from God. No, it is referring to one's money gift. The king didn't just see anybody. He saw people based on the gift they brought him, but that's another teaching.

One-sided Relationships vs. Mutually Beneficial Relationships

David arrives at the king's castle and begins to play for Saul, and the evil spirit of Satan departs from him. Why did it leave? David was anointed. He is a bridge to Saul, not a burden. In the midst of all that was happening, King Saul only wants David in his presence for one reason, to deliver him. There was nothing in it for David. Their relationship was one-sided.

One-sided relationships are not of God because they are burdens. Everything in King Saul and David's relationship was to Saul's advantage. David was merely being used. Let me explain something to you about usury. You can be used so long that you begin to enjoy it. You won't mind it, especially if you are being used by the right person, and you believe your willingness to be taken advantage of will keep them in your life. Beloved, that's no kind of life to live. If someone is using you only for what you have, for what they can get out of you, that is not the kind of life God wants you to live. God wants you to be in relationships that are mutually productive. My sister, it does not matter how a man may make your ego rise, or how a woman may make your ego inflate, my brother, God wants you in relationships that are *mutually* productive, not one-sided. Not something for one and nothing for the other.

I had to take inventory of my life at one point in time; I began to question myself about my associates. I began to ask why they were in my life. It may be time to do inventory of your friends and clean some of them out of your life, if they are burdens. Start asking the question, "Why are you here?"

I had to do this from time to time with people who would call me on the telephone. "Why am I talking to you? Is this going to be beneficial? If so, I'll continue to talk, but if it will not benefit me, why am I wasting all of my time talking to you? There is nothing in this for me." Many people have never been taught this before. They were taught to be available to benefit someone else. God did not make you to be the savior; He is the savior. He places people in your life to benefit you, and He places you in the lives of people so you can benefit them.

So when you ask the question, "Why are you here?," you will begin to qualify your friends. Some of you may find it necessary to ask more direct questions, "Why are you troubling me?" and "What do you want?" These questions cut to the heart of the matter so that any underlying motives may be seen before a relationship is developed. Find out if it is going to be mutually beneficial. Ask yourself, if you are giving all of yourself without receiving anything in return, why is that individual in your life?

Some parents have 40-year-old and older children who still are siphoning off of them. They need to ask, "Why are you still bothering me? Why am I still supporting you?" After they've spent a significant period of time helping their adult children gain economic footing, parents have to cut them off. Adult children begin supporting themselves, even if it means mom and dad have to set an ultimatum.

I like nature's story of the mother eagle and her eaglets. She takes care of them from the time she lays her eggs and nurtures them until they hatch. In the nest, she creates a mechanism that has the psychological effect of forcing them to become independent after reaching a certain stage of growth. The first layer of the nest is a soft, cottony, cushioned bed. The bed is supported by a foundation, and under the foundation she creates a layer of thorns, briers, and other kinds of prickly objects. When the eaglets are young, their weight is very light. They are in the cottony part "living large," "maxin' and relaxin." They're enjoying themselves, waiting for their mother to bring the next meal. As they begin to grow a little bit more, their weight increases and they sink downward. The bed is still kind of soft and cottony, but not as it once was. As the mother continues feeding her eaglets, they get a little heavier, then swoosh! They push down to the third level where the prickly briers and the thorns are sticking them. When they push all the way down with their rear ends, there is only one response, *jump up and fly out!*

Some people need to bring thorns into their relationships. Some of the people who are in your life should jump up and fly. One thing people misunderstand as they enter into relationships is that they do not have to have open communication with everyone who expresses an interest in them. I have asked some people, "Well, why are you talking to this person?" Their response is, "Because they talked to me." That response is similar to the one some people give for always answering the telephone: "Because it rings." That's the wrong philosophy. If you pay the telephone bill, you have the option of allowing it to ring until Jesus returns. You are under no obligation to answer it. Answering it is a choice. The same thing applies to answering the door at your home. You do not have to answer it every time someone comes. That is why a little spy glass was installed in some doors, so you can decide whether or not it is somebody you want to be bothered with. You go to the door and say, "Ah, that's Ralph. He talks too long; he doesn't know when to go home." You go and get back in your bed. You don't have to answer the door.

This same philosophy applies to relationships. You do not have to become involved with everyone who comes along. I certainly hope that women understand this. Give yourself some time to watch a man's behavior before committing to him. Some women get so desperate and think, "Jesus, if he just looks like he's going to pass by this way, I'm going to stop him! 'Cause that's my blessing!"

Whoa! If God is on your side, and He already told you He is what you need, then He is going to send you who you need. Elijah applied this principle to Elisha (II Kings 2:1-6). He attempted thrice to get him to reveal his true self by acting as though he (Elijah) did not want him (Elisha) to follow him. From this lesson, we learn not to be so quick in accepting people before determining if they are a bridge or a burden.

The Spirit of Jealousy in Relationships

Turn to I Samuel 18:6. I am going to show you how the relationship changes between David and Saul. As you read this passage, notice how God was working with David even though Saul was taking advantage of him. God was yet blessing David in the kingdom.

He traveled back and forth from the castle to his home. David would remain with the king for a few days, go back home and stay with his father, and return to play for Saul. Then the giant, Goliath, rose up as an enemy to the people of God. One of the times David was at home, he heard about the threat of Goliath. In I Samuel 17:32-39, he goes back to the palace to serve Saul and tells him he's going to fight the giant. When Saul tries to give him his armament, David says, "I've not proved this so I don't need it. It's too heavy for me. I'm just going to take what I have, the sling shot and five smooth stones." In I Samuel 18:6-7, David has returned from the battle where he has just wiped out Israel's chief enemy, Goliath. "And it came to pass as they came, when David was returned from the slaughter of the Philistine, that the women came out of all cities of Israel, singing and dancing, to meet King Saul, with tabrets, with joy, and instruments of music. And the women answered one another as they played, and said, 'Saul has slain his thousands, and David his ten thousands.'"

Now, if a person is in relationship with you for the right reasons, if God has placed them in your life for the right reasons, then they will not mind when you are recognized and elevated. As a matter of fact, they will celebrate when you are recognized. They will not be jealous of you.

At my church, I usually tell everyone to say "click" before giving information that may be a bit strong. It is the sound of your spiritual seatbelt being fastened in preparation for a collision with the truth. So say "click" before reading the following paragraph.

You are a fool if you marry or enter into any relationship with an insanely jealous person. (I told you it was going to be strong.) You are a fool, and I will tell you why. That is a fool you're in relationship with and it takes a fool to marry or associate with one, especially when you already know what type of characteristics the person possesses. They already have demonstrated violent behavior toward you just because it appeared someone else was gaining ground with you. They cursed the wallpaper off the wall, jumped on the person or assassinated their character, and hit you in the eye and it's draining. You now have a black circle around it, and you weren't even committed to them!

You say they love you. If someone is physically abusive before marriage or a commitment, you should show them two things: the biggest board you can find to break it over their skull and your backside as you're moving away. Take these drastic actions. Relationships such as marriage are challenging enough. If they react to situations in that manner during courtship, it is only going to accelerate afterwards.

If someone opens their mouth to verbally attack you, it only is a matter of time before it becomes physical or diabolical. Some people who have been physically abused know that what I'm saying is true. If they are disrespectful enough to curse you, they will knock you out. This is the new millennium and there are some women who will fight. Brothers, this warning applies to you as well. If a woman will curse you out, then she will knock you out.

Parents, some of you are in relationship with children who are hitting you. There should be a contest for children who have physically abused their parents called *Where is the child now?* Is that a child or is that ground beef? Those are the only things we should have to answer.

So now, a person in a mutually beneficial relationship rejoices when their partner is exalted. That can be something as simple as one person receiving a promotion on a job that causes him or her to make more money. The other person should not have a problem with it. If the female spouse earns more money than her counterpart, then bring it on. The male should not have a problem with it. When he goes to the store, they do not ask who earned the money; they just ask, "Can you afford it?"

Some men have difficulty accepting their wives earning higher salaries, because they were taught that they are the man of the house. Some men also believe that as long as their wife looks unkept, they do not have to be concerned about anyone else being attracted to them. When the wife starts coming out, all of a sudden he has pressing concerns. When she looked like an accident looking for a place to happen, there was no problem. Now, she dresses up, and don't let her spray some perfume on when she never used to. "Ah, you got somebody, don't you? I know you got somebody. You're wearing that for somebody else." Her response should be, "No, that's not necessarily true, I just found out who I am. Your tired self didn't help me get anywhere. So now I'm getting ready to look all right for me!"

Do not let anyone keep you in bondage. When you are in relationship with people, it should always be progressive. It should be going higher and higher. One of the things that really bothers me is when a man marries a woman, and the woman's appearance goes down. She looked good before she married him, and now she looks horrible. Any man in his right mind should want something nice to look at, praise the Lord.

Earlier in this book, I gave an example of a wife who takes her appearance for granted because her husband doesn't complain to her about it. "My husband likes me like this." Okay, watch who he is looking at when he is not looking at you, and you will find out what he really likes. "He likes me homely." I bet he is not looking at homely women on the street. He's looking at those nice long legs and little skirt. But there you are looking like Whoopie Goldberg's character, "Celie" in the movie "The Color Purple" and thinking he likes the way you look.

Jealousy Turns a Bridge into a Burden

Going back to our scriptural reference, Chapter 18 and Verse 8, let's look at how Saul's jealousy prompted him to behave when the women sang praises of David's accomplishments. "Saul was very angry for the saying displeased him . . . ." Why is he so displeased? He is jealous. King Solomon says that jealousy is as cruel as the grave. The Bible says in Proverbs 14:30, " . . . and envy, the rottenness of the bones." Some people are so duped by the spirit of jealousy that they confuse it with love. "He is so jealous of me because he loves me." No, no, no! That is a demon, and it is going to be a matter of time before he shows you just how much under the power of Satan he is.

I never liked jealous people. I am too outgoing. I told my wife before we were married, "If you're going to be a jealous woman, let me just leave you where you are." You cannot work for the Lord and be involved with a jealous person. As a minister, people are around me all of the time. Therefore, it is necessary that all parties connected with me are bridge-minded and not selfish. I am not a jealous person. My wife can do whatever she wants to, and I don't ask her when she is coming back, unless it is going to be dark or some situation like that. If she wants to go shopping, fine. If I had concerns about it, I would have never married her.

If you are not in a relationship where you can trust the other person, you might as well pull out of it. A spirit of jealousy is not going to keep your partner from doing what they want to do. You see, you have to put some things to rest while you are still in the dating stage. If you did not put those concerns to rest during the courtship, then leave them alone. Love thinketh no ill of its neighbor, and the first neighbor you have is the closest person you are in relationship with. As you live and as time keeps moving on, sisters, there are going to be a lot of other women passing by your man who look a whole lot better than you. I will be honest and say that he may be watching them. Remember, however, you are going home with him, praise the Lord.

Brothers, as you get older there are going to be many younger men who look better than you ever thought you looked, and your wife may look at them. My wife already has shown me her ideal man. I asked her, "Why isn't that me?" We saw a man one night on television and I said, "That's him right there!" She looked at me and said, "Yes sir, that's him." I asked, "Why isn't it me?" She answered, "Oh, you're just a little bit off, not far off." I said, "Yeah right." I could look at the man and see the difference between him and me. I was not that crazy, ego and all.

Seek God for the Bridge You Need

What I am trying to help you understand is that every relationship you become involved in may not be ideal, but it should be beneficial. If it is from God, your spouse may not be the type of person you've always envisioned you would have. The average person will not marry their ideal person. Young people who have not matured live in a fantasy world. When you become mature, you realize many of your concepts and previously held desires were fantasies. They were not realistic. What a person wants and needs is as distant and different as the Atlantic and Pacific oceans. Think about it for a moment. Think about the man you wanted, sister, and the one you are in relationship with. The best thing to do as you compare your dream with reality is laugh. Unmarried women, think about the man you idealistically want and the one you've been dating. Men, think about the woman you envisioned yourself being in a love affair with. Recall the woman, brothers, you were imagining in your fantasy hour, and think about who was really there when you opened your eyes. There's a difference.

Are we on the same page now? You see, beloved, there is a stark difference between what a person wants and what a person needs. What one wants typically is pleasing to the eye and the mind. What one needs will be mutually beneficial. It is time that we begin to enter into relationships with a produced benefit. You do not work on a job without benefits, so then why are you entering into relationships without any benefits? Some people who are unmarried should ask, "What is beneficial about me to the end that someone will desire me?" If you have nothing beneficial, then why are you complaining about being alone? Okay, ask yourself a different question. "What separates me from another single person just like me?" "What distinguishes me?"

A key word I learned in business while I was working secularly is the term "marketable." We used to teach people that you have to have marketable skills. In other words, you have to be able to perform tasks which merit payment. If you cannot, then you will not be in a position to receive a paycheck.

Some people want a job that pays them thousands of dollars a year, but they cannot even type or use a computer. I want to know what marketable skills you possess? This also applies to relationships. What makes a person marketable? What makes a man or a woman desirable? In the body of Christ, a lot of us sing the same songs and share similar experiences because of our faith, but what has God done in your life that distinguishes you from someone else just like you? Please do not refer to a physical characteristic or ability in your answer. A person has to be married for only two weeks to understand that this was a fallacy. What you can do in the bedroom will not hold a relationship together, because once the other person learns all of your moves, it will be as if you are caught in a time warp. If you've ever loved a particular decade, then you will know what I'm talking about. Some people love the '70s, but as much as they may love that period, they must realize that time has moved on. A person can live in that era if it pleases them, but time has moved on. They can try to sing all the songs of the '70s, but a lot of people will not know what they are singing about. That is the way your relationship will be if you base it solely on the physical aspect. It will be a "has-been."

The Jealousy of a Burden Will Attempt to Destroy the Bridge

If a person is jealous of you, it will only be a matter of time until they attempt to hurt you in some way. Verses 8-9 state, ". . . Saul was very angry, for the saying displeased him; and he said, 'They have ascribed unto David ten thousands and to me they have ascribed only thousands: and what more can he have but the kingdom?' And Saul jealously eyed David from that point forward."

Let's look at Verse 10, a passage I previously discussed. "The next day an evil spirit from God came mightily upon Saul, and he raved madly in the house while David played the lyre with his hands, as at other times, and there was a javelin in Saul's hand . . . ."

David entered into a relationship that was not mutually beneficial. Saul began to extract his gift, taking advantage of the gift by manipulating him. David was not receiving anything from Saul, but was promoted nonetheless. Saul became more and more angry. He was jealous of David and prepared to hurt him.

If you have ever been hurt or disappointed in a relationship, it probably was because you were involved with someone who was not mutually producing benefit as you were to them. You see, beloved, there are persons who do not value what they do not pay for. A person usually values what they pay for or invest in. One has to be psychotic to deface what they've paid for. When you buy a car, you're not going to tear it down. If a person invests into your life, they are not going to be the one to tear you down. If they are stripping everything like a strip miner, after they're finished, you won't be good for anything.

I have seen women who have had all kinds of potential in them, and in a few years they became involved with a "strip miner" (burden), and gave up. Their beauty and personality were gone. All of their desirable attributes had diminished. They were stripped down and left with nothing. All they were good for then was for people to pass by, saying what used to be.

In Verse 11, we'll continue looking at the behavior of a jealous person. "And Saul cast the javelin, for he thought, I will pin David to the wall, and David evaded him twice." Look at this. Here's a man who has benefitted by David's relationship. David has been a bridge to him—a bridge from insanity into sanity. Yet he has become so dispossessed and displaced by jealousy, that he tries to terminate the thing that's a bridge to him. What many don't understand about a relationship is that if you're not benefitting from it, the person who is extracting both your anointing and your gift from you will sooner or later try to destroy you. It's a natural process even though you are being beneficial to them. Why? They are not giving anything. Relationships are designed to be based on giving and receiving, and when one person is doing all giving without receiving, or all receiving without giving, destruction is imminent.

Saul was under the influence of jealousy so deeply that he didn't think about what he would do if David was not around when the evil spirit was on him. He thought David was *replaceable*, "I'll just get somebody else to play for me." When you are in a relationship that God did not ordain, your partner will think you are replaceable! That person does not see any value in you. In other words, as grandmother used to say, "You will be taken for granted."

Behave Wisely with a Burden . . . And You'll Win

The Spirit of God was no longer with Saul (I Samuel 16:13-14). He now resided with David. Saul was afraid of David. He became so fearful that in Verse 13 that he removes him from his presence. David became Saul's commander over a thousand, and no longer personally ministered to his emotional needs.

Have you ever been moved out of your place as David was? The position seemed to be yours initially, but someone grew tired of you and moved you to another area, putting you over something else, with someone else. For example, you had babies for them, but now they merely want you to take care of the children. They don't want you for the love affair anymore, just to take care of the children. Much of this could have been avoided if the relationship initially was mutually beneficial. The goal of this relationship should be to have someone who is a true bridge. Not only are they supporting you, but there also is a great need for the relationship to be free of jealousy, which comes as a result of a non-mutually beneficial arrangement. Proverbs 14:30 states that "envy (jealousy) is the rottenness of the bones." The destruction or ruin of any relationship is the void of mutual benefit.

So David was moved from ministering to Saul and made military commander over a thousand. In Verses 13 and 14, David chooses to win the grand prize. He is the perfect example of how to respond to a burden's attack. "And he went out and came in before the people. And David behaved himself wisely in all his ways; and the Lord was with him." I like David because he was a bridge. He acted wisely in all of his ways and succeeded. So even if a person has displaced you, do not act out of character. Do not let it destroy you. What one person did not realize in you, someone else will.

There is somebody else who will not leave you. Why should you care if someone doesn't love you anymore? There are too many people out there, and you probably will happen upon someone who will be better to you than the last one. Some people want to commit suicide by jumping off a cliff. Move on. For some of you, the divorce is over. Move on. You have papers and they have turned yellow. That is one indication to you that you need to move on. The babies that you had now have babies. That is a good indication that you need to move on. You may say to your former mate, "You were my first love, but now I'm a grandparent. Honey, I need to move on." Don't get stuck in a rut just because one person doesn't desire you. Move on. Go out and come in. Behave yourself wisely and don't give up. Don't get out of character. Even if you have to deal with the situation of divorce, whether it be from a marriage or a position or a business arrangement, don't let it devastate you. Okay, so that one did not work out. At least don't get into another situation just like the one you just left.

Look at Saul's observation of David. Verse 15 (Amplified Bible) reads, "When Saul saw how capable David was, he stood in awe of him." That is how successful he was. Many of us need to learn from David's example. If someone doesn't desire you anymore, then improve yourself as much as you possibly can. Become more refined and appealing in every way! Purchase new clothes, makeup your face a little differently (if this applies), get your hair done—

right. Let people see what they missed out on. You have to let them know that it's not over for you. You need to have this mind-set toward them, "Just 'cause you didn't want me doesn't mean no one else wants me!" They will do exactly what King Saul did; he stood in awe of David. He said, "I don't like the boy, but he has something on him. Something is blessing him. I wish I wouldn't have let him go." If they pursue you with those words, tell them, "Your eyes may water, your teeth may grit, but this one person you'll never get!"

As Saul's jealousy intensified, David continued to gain praise from the people, even the entire nation. Verse 16: "But all Israel and Judah loved David, for he went out and came in . . . ." One of the things you must understand is that the recognition and elevation of one can change the other into a burden. In other words, the bridge can change into a burden if a spirit of jealousy is in them. Jealousy can change a relationship. "Pastor, they changed." No, they did not. You simply did not allow enough time to see what was really in them. If you had given the relationship the appropriate amount of time, you would have seen that there is a spirit in that person that is not going to be conducive to a good relationship or mutually beneficial. If you're being good to them, then they need to be good to you.

CHAPTER 4

Mutually Beneficial Relationships

In this chapter, we will take a closer look at David and King Saul's relationship, and I will show you how David continued to be a bridge to Saul even though Saul was a burden. At this point, however, I want to discuss the term "mutually beneficial" in more detail.

Relationships that are ordained of God should be mutually beneficial or bilateral. In other words, it should be good for all parties involved. A win-win situation. Everyone is getting something measurable out of it. It is enjoyable to all involved. Another way of saying it is, "I will do some of the things you want to do, and you will do some of the things I want to do, even though I may not like it."

I used to believe that once you are married, you and your spouse automatically begin to like the same things. I presumed you would never disagree over things such as disliking what your spouse enjoys. What are you going to do when you're supposed to be spending quality time together, but hate the kind of television program your partner enjoys?

You can do what I did, snatch the remote and tell them, "I'm the king of this castle and this is what we're going to watch!" You can do this, but I promise you the relationship will not be a lasting or enjoyable one. Your spouse will sit on the side, miserable. Take it from one who knows, if your spouse is miserable, it will only be a very small fragment of time before you will begin to experience the same kind of misery, on a different level. If you are a married man, please heed these words: "If mama ain't happy, fix whatever it is she ain't happy about." Those are words to the wise. Women, if your husband is not happy, find out what it will take to make him happy and repair it. Spouses can isolate you in ways that can cause grief on another level! Your wife doesn't have to say anything to you; she'll just put ice on you. Women can isolate their husbands to such a degree that they'll be ready to convert: "Okay, I repent! I repent! What is it? I repent, just forgive me." No one told me there would be days like this. So when you are dealing with people in any kind of relationship, the goal should be mutually beneficial. That means selfishness never has a place. Although it always will try to resurrect its head, it has no place in your relationships.

Remaining in an "Unequally Yoked" Relationship?

Let's examine another aspect of a bilateral or mutually beneficial relationship. Saul was trying to kill David, yet David was still being a blessing to him. How long should a person remain in a relationship like this one?

Here is a particularly common situation. Two people in a courtship are lost in sin. They are having a good time frequenting the nightclub circuit and so forth. Then, one of them gets saved, receiving the message of Jesus Christ. That person will be fine, but a lot of trouble will begin for the other individual. Eventually, it will breakdown the relationship because the couple is not doing the same things anymore.

So here you are saved, having received the baptism of the Holy Spirit. You have that power inside of you now, but the person you're involved with still is in love with the devil. You attend church alone because your partner does not share your mind-set. You don't want to go to the nightclub with him or her because you don't share their mind-set.

Let me digress for a moment and say this: I refuse to perform wedding ceremonies for unequally yoked couples who are in this type of predicament. I do not have a problem marrying two sinners, and I definitely have no problem with two Christians coming into a marital relationship. I do have concerns when one individual is saved and the other is not. It's going to take some special kind of love because it's such a rare thing for this kind of relationship to work.

What happens if you already are married and things go in this direction? You have to be thinking, "What am I going to do? How long should I continue being a blessing to this person, a bridge to this burden?" You also can apply this question to other areas of your life. How long should I stay on this job, giving it 100 percent when it only returns 10 percent to me? How long should I continue to fast, pray, and seek God, when it seems like I'm getting nothing out of the deal? How long should I give my tithes and offerings, not seeing any returns, before I decide to keep all of my money? The question on the table is, "How long?"

There are some relationships that seem to be burdensome, yet they have the potential for change. There are other relationships that are burdensome that do not have the potential for change. You may be right there in the midst of the valley of decision, wondering which of the two your relationship falls in.

To deal specifically with the marital relationship, let's read I Corinthians 7:7, "For I would that all men were even as I myself. But every man has his proper gift of God, one after this manner, and another after that."

What "gift" was the Apostle Paul referring to? Paul was gifted by God to be a eunuch. He was not homosexual or an embittered divorcee, nor did he have a hate for women due to physical abuse by his mother. He was not sexist; he was a eunuch. There were three types of eunuchs described in the Bible (St. Matthew 9:12). One type was a man who received a special grace gifting from God to reserve his entire life for God's use. The Holy Spirit was able to flow through him without external hindrances. He did not desire to complicate the activity of God in his life with a domestic relationship, which carries its own set of responsibilities.

Allow me to point out what is meant by the term "external hindrances." For instance, I am a pastor, ordained to be used of

God. Because I have a wife, my role as a husband carries a set of duties. Sometimes I put ministry-related work aside and minister to her needs as a woman. Sometimes she needs attention; she gets broken (it's a good broken), and I have to repair her. Sometimes I'm broken and she needs to leave what she is doing to repair me. I have to drop everything at times to repair this and that in my family. I have to stop working for the Lord to deal with my children. If you ignore such situations, they're just going to go their own way.

People need to bear in mind that we are living in a day when marriages are very different from those 30 years ago. For many, this is not the first marriage, and some people even have children from previous relationships. Thus, people enter into marriage with additional weight-bearing obligations. These duties, if left unaddressed, can hinder a person's growth in the Lord. In contrast to myself, that type of eunuch was anointed to have no physical desires for the opposite sex, no interference of the natural, in order to be better used by God.

Then there was another kind of eunuch who was one by choice. A person who had become so engrossed with the love and power of God and with the demonstration of the Holy Spirit, that they decided to give themselves fully to the work of the Lord. They didn't need any other distractions and were able to live without a woman.

If you try going this route and emotions rise inside of you, that is not your anointing. If you wake up in the morning and still have a desire for the opposite gender, that is not your anointing. So get out of that mind-set. We will deal with that specific situation in verse 9.

The third eunuch was a man who had been castrated. Most of these men were confiscated from other countries during war and taken to serve the king and his people. The purpose of the castration was to demonstrate enslavement and also to ensure there would be no mixing of the slaves' seed throughout the kingdom. These eunuchs did not concern themselves with marriage because they had no desire for women any longer.

The Apostle Paul was the type of eunuch to whom God had given a specific gift that enabled him to devote himself fully to a divine call. The power of God flowed through his life with no outside interruption.

The Amplified Bible says in I Corinthians 7:7-8, "I wish that all brothers were just like me." We see that Paul had a wish that did not come true! He was not using his faith, okay?, this was only a wish. "I am in this manner of self-control, but each has his own special gift from God." Don't get upset if you do not have the gift that the Apostle Paul operated in. God will give you another one. "But to the unmarried people and the widows (and I'm going to add the divorced to this category), I declare that it is well, it is good, advantageous, expedient, and awesome for them to remain single, even as I do myself."

Paul says that you are in a better position to serve God when you are single. You might not be in a better position as it relates to controlling your emotions and your physical desires, but as it relates to serving God, you can serve Him a whole lot better without extra baggage.

Let's continue reading Verse 9, "But, if they have not self-control (restraint of their passions), they should get married." Who are the people who should get married? Christians who have a desire. Women, if you do not like men, be honest with yourself. Don't let the word "married" come out of your mouth if you truly do not want to be in a lifelong physical relationship with a man. Marriage is for those who have passion. If you are a woman who says, "I don't like him to touch me. He just touches me and something goes all through me," then you are not the marrying type. "I'm going to change," you may say. More than likely, you will not. Stay single, because you will divorce. A man is marrying you for a lot of touching—for life. He's never going to get delivered from that one thing. You can't cast that devil out; it's in him for good. Jesus will not take it from him, because he is going to need it later especially if you leave him. You see, another woman will appreciate it.

So marriage is for people who have a physical and emotional desire on the inside of them that is bottled up, and it needs to be released for someone else who has a like passion. I know some sisters who do not have a problem with this aspect of a relationship. They understand it perfectly. Most people get married for that reason only, to put the fire out. "Honey, it's just a blaze. It's been blazing so much that it's burned up all kinds of timber—valuable timber. And now, I'm just ready to have the fire put out!" They may be thinking, "When can you put the fire out? How soon can it be extinguished?" You want it out quickly, and you want a person who has the ability to do so. This is noble, as Verse 9 says, "It is better to marry than to be aflame with passion and tortured continually with ungratified desire." This is true. Amen. It is better to marry and have someone who can put the fire out, not fan the flame. Some people don't know what to look for in a mate, and they are not allowing the Holy Spirit to guide them to the person with whom they are compatible. You think you're getting an extinguisher, but you're really getting a gasoline tank. They only make the fire hotter and rage and burn more intensely because they cannot put it out. Some people get upset and almost backslide in their bedroom because they need their passion satisfied. Their incompatible partner can't fulfill the need.

God is going to lead you. It is His responsibility to lead you to the one whom He has ordained to put your fire out. Everyone can't do it, even with the necessary equipment. God has ordained certain people with the right chemistry to come into your life and help you in the area of sexual fulfillment. There are certain chemical elements that can put mature fires out, and there are others that exacerbate the problem. It is the same way in your body.

> "It is better to marry than to be aflame with passion and tortured continually with ungratified desire. But to the married people, I give charge, not I, but the Lord, that the wife is not to separate from her husband: but and if she depart . . . ." (I Corinthians 7:9-11).

Many people depart marriages because of the lack of information. Everyone has not been privileged to receive the correct kind of teaching so that they can make good choices as it relates to the right mate. Sometimes, with incorrect teaching, you end up with the wrong mate in a disastrous relationship that will not correct itself. Remember, the question on the table is, "How long should you be in a relationship that is not mutually or bilaterally productive?"

I have even started teaching my sons the kind of woman to look for. I tell them, "You can't marry just any woman. Don't give just 'any' young lady your phone number! There's a special kind of woman you're looking for. 'Any' woman is everywhere and may not have what is required to fulfill your needs. You don't take this kind of person home to live with you." It's one kind of person that is used over and over again like a sponge, but it's another kind that you will marry. That's not right, but that's the way it is. When you get those confused and take the street partner home with you, it almost never works out.

Let's continue with the remainder of Verse 11, " . . . but and if she depart, let her remain unmarried, or be reconciled to her husband. And let not the husband put away his wife." God is saying, here you are in a relationship, and it's not beneficial for both parties. That's the "but and if she (or he) departs" portion of the scripture. What are the grounds for departure? No. 1, scripture is clear about fornication and adultery. Allow me to offer some other gray areas that qualify for departure as well.

Lack of compatibility is a major area of confusion which could result in a reason for someone leaving any type of relationship. That compatibility, or the lack thereof, could begin with one being Christian and the other being non-Christian. In a lot of cases, the relationship will not work. And after you have done as much as lieth in you to live peaceably with that person (Romans 12:18), and peace does not come of it, then begin to seek God for the solution. Now every solution is not the same. God will tell some people to stay in there. To other people, God will say to come out. You have to seek Him to find out when your time is up.

In other times, the lack of compatibility can be something as simple as having or being the wrong person. Let's deal with this for a moment by reviewing Verse 11, "but and if she depart, let her remain unmarried, or be reconciled to her husband. And let not the husband put away his wife." First of all, divorce has never been God's design. Never. He said because of the hardness of people's hearts, Moses wrote letters of divorcement so one could separate from the other (St. Matthew 19:5-9). Under the law, that same letter of divorcement stated that a person who came out of a relationship could not enter into another one. That person had to be celibate throughout life. That was the understanding of divorcement.

When you divorce and marry someone else, in God's perfect order, it is sin. You violated His commandment. What is sin except breaking the commandments of God? Here is what we teach:

"Divorce" sin is forgivable when one repents and changes. If you have committed this sin, say, "Father, in the name of Jesus, I confess my sin, and Lord lead me to the person that is going to put my fire out and be a bridge to me."

Divorce is a sin or missing of the mark just like any other sin, but God is in the forgiving business. Think about it, He already knew you were going to sin. For this reason, he underwrote forgiveness into the provision of grace. I John 1:9 says, "If we confess our sins, He is faithful and just to forgive us our sins, and to cleanse us from all unrighteousness." This includes divorce. So, be free from guilt. The beauty of that kind of situation is when God forgives, He forgives as if the occurrence never happened. When this "forgiven" person prepares to marry, in God's eyes it is as if they never were married. He wiped all of the old stuff away. That is why you have to put it in the category of sin so you can receive atonement for it. He washed it all away. He said, "Your sins and your iniquities, I will remember no more" (Hebrews 8:12; 10:17). It is as if it never happened. Now you can stand before God's holy altar and take a vow with another individual as if you never did before. That's great, isn't it?

I am still addressing how long one is to remain in a non-fulfilling relationship. In I Corinthians 7:12, Paul says, "But to the rest speak I, not the Lord: if any brother have a wife that believeth not, and she be pleased to dwell with him, let him not put her away."

You get born-again, and receive Jesus and begin walking by faith and not by sight. You're going to church all the time, praying in the Holy Spirit, reading the Word of God, and the person you're married to says, "Uh, uh, I love you, I don't care. I'm going to hang in here." The Word says to let your unsaved spouse stay. Under this condition, there isn't any Biblical law or scripture that advocates divorce. Because you received salvation, it does not mean you can tell your mate, "Old things have passed away, and *you* are the old thing." That is not what the Lord had in mind.

The Bible gives the person who is not "in the light" the option of remaining in the marriage or leaving. In this respect, the Christian does not have an option. The Word of God says that if the unsaved spouse wants to boogie and leave, then let them go. If they stay, something supernatural has the potential of happening. You see,

God is always in the business of equity, bridge with bridge or burden with burden. If the marriage consists of a bridge and a burden, God intends to do something to change the burden into a bridge, or else it will be an unequally yoked situation. This is the opposite of the phrase "mutually beneficial." When you're saved, you are covered under the blood of Jesus and qualify to receive divine protection from God. That anointing will make something supernatural happen in your life. Once you're in relationship with God, He is going to touch the rest of your relationships.

Verse 13 says, "And the woman which hath an husband that believeth not, and if he be pleased to dwell with her, let her not leave him." So it is the same stroke for both genders.

Before continuing further, I must emphasize that this scripture only applies to husbands and wives. If you are not married, then you are free to leave your partner. Do not bring the bridge or burden into a marriage. If you get born-again and your significant other does not want to, you are supposed to dissolve the relationship, no matter how good it has been. You are in light and that person is in darkness. What most people try to do is bring the dark person into the marvelous light, and the individual won't fit unless salvation takes place!

Let's read Verse 14 in the Amplified Bible. It says, "For the unbelieving husband is set apart, separated, withdrawn from heathen contamination and affiliated with Christian people by union with his consecrated and set-apart wife." In other words, the unsaved spouse will be influenced by the light of God in the saved one's life. As the spouse in darkness chooses to remain married, his or her spirit will be influenced with the light of the gospel present in the house. God begins to make a change. The spouse in darkness begins to desire to walk after God. They willed to stay and passed the test. God's Word is saying if the unsaved desires to remain, then it is only a matter of time before he or she desires to be with Him.

However, this only applies to married people. If you are not married, require your potential spouse to either cross the line where you are and get saved (become a bridge), or stay on the other side (remain a burden), and get back. That is how relationships work. Some people believe a child of light can date a child of darkness. It doesn't work. What communication does light have with darkness?

When you turn the lights on in your home, what happens with darkness? It dissipates or disappears. This is the same relationship you should have with unfruitful works of darkness. When you show up, if they are in darkness, they ought to disappear.

In marriage, some Christians have problems when their unsaved spouse no longer desires to be with them. The Bible makes it very plain what to do in this case. Verse 15 says, "But if the unbelieving partner actually leaves, let him do so. In such cases, the remaining brother or sister is not morally bound, but God has called us to peace." If they decide to leave, let them go. They don't want to remain because you are walking with Jesus now. Let them go. The law has released you and you are free now. You can marry anybody the Lord sends to you, even if you have to initiate the divorce process. If they leave and say, "Well I'm just not going to file the appropriate papers," *you* have the right to file them. At times, Christians are afraid to file divorce papers. File them. If they left, they are gone.

God has called you to peace, so do not grieve over something that is over. Don't let your mind be frustrated by it. Read further, "For wife, how can you be sure of converting and saving your husband, or husband how can you be sure of converting and saving your wife? Only let each one seek to conduct himself and regulate his affairs, so as to lead the life which the Lord has allotted and imparted to him, and to which God has invited and summoned him; that is my order in all the churches." He says that if you lead the life God has called you to, it will touch the person that is in relationship with you. If they will to change, then God will change them. If they will to leave, then let them go.

Now finally, to answer the "how long" question, when you are a bridge and you have received a burden in exchange, God says, "Seek me. I'll give you the time." If you are not married, dissolve the relationship and explain to the person that he or she will have to develop a right relationship with God, then the two of you will discuss progressing as a couple. It is that simple.

Would you knowingly buy a house that is damaged? That is so against nature that there are laws prohibiting this. If a person sells a house knowing something is wrong with it and doesn't disclose it before selling it, you can take them to court and get out of the mortgage agreement. It's against principle. Well, why is it that people are continuously entering into relationships with others they know have things wrong with them? The basic thing is, they are in sin and nothing is going to fly right in the relationship. Give them a choice, get saved or get lost. It's cold, but not as cold as it will be if you marry them.

Burdens Destroy Mutually Beneficial Relationships

Now we're going to return to I Samuel to take a look at the bridge David made himself to be while Saul chose to burden him. Let's read the following passages of scripture: "And as David returned from the slaughter of the Philistine, Abner took him, and brought him before Saul with the head of the Philistine in his hand. And Saul said to him, 'Whose son art thou, young man?' And David answered, 'I am the son of thy servant Jesse the Bethlehemite.'" (I Samuel 17:57). "And David went out whithersoever Saul sent him, and behaved himself wisely: and Saul set him over the men of war, and he was accepted in the sight of all the people, and also in the sight of Saul's servants" (I Samuel 18:5). "And David behaved himself wisely in all his ways; and the Lord was with him" (I Samuel 18:14).

David is the bridge to Saul; he is a blessing to him. He behaves himself wisely. In every affair Saul has, David does the right thing. Not only that, he has indentured himself as a servant to Saul. He literally waits on him hand and foot. He is a blessing to him. He is a bridge. Look again at what happens to Saul when David receives recognition for killing Goliath.

"And it came to pass as they came, as David was returned from the slaughter of the Philistine, that the women came out of all the cities of Israel, singing and dancing to meet King Saul with tabrets, with joy with instruments of music, and the women answered one another as they played and said, 'Saul has slain his thousands and David his ten thousands;' and Saul was very wroth, and the saying displeased him, and he said, 'They have ascribed unto David ten thousands, and to me ascribed but thou-

sands, and what can he have more, but the kingdom?'
And Saul eyed David from that day forward" (I Samuel
18:6-9).

When you are involved in a relationship with someone and you
constantly are blessing, bridging, and giving that person favor, yet
they only extrapolate from you, take from you, and never give, then
it is not of God. It's only going to lead to a downfall. It will only be
a matter of time before the relationship suffers destruction.

In a mutually beneficial relationship, David gave himself to serve
Saul, and Saul should have given himself to serve David. If David
says, "I'm going to behave myself wisely as it relates to your
affairs," then Saul should have behaved himself wisely as it related
to David's affairs. Like David, you are a Christian person doing the
right thing, and the person you're involved with keeps doing the
wrong thing to you. Seek God because there may be a door out of
that relationship.

Sometimes people tell you things without saying a word. With
their actions, they tell you they no longer want to be in the relationship and they are ready to move on, but they are just not mature
enough to verbally tell you that it's over. You need to be able to
look at their behavior and attention level toward you and say, "Well
you know what? This is over." Think about it. You are trying to do
everything this person has asked you to, and you're trying to do it
correctly. They have asked you to back them up and told you they
would back you up as well. Every time you need your back
covered, it gets broken. Every time they need a loan, you lend them
money, but when you need a little assistance, you can't find them.
They know your distress calls and they never answer you. They
know that when you call at a certain time, you are in need of money,
and they get lost. If you're giving to them, they should give back. If
you are buying lunch all the time, every now and then they should
buy a dinner or a Snickers bar. My God, just bring something!

You can gauge where you stand in relationships based on what
people do, not what they say. Keep this in mind: love is action.

It used to amaze me to see how a man could get a normally lucid,
rational thinking woman turned on to drugs. After she became
addicted, he prostituted her body on the streets. The relationship

appeared to have a good start. Both smoked dope together, but in his mind, he is preparing her for whoredom on the street. In her mind, she's thinking, "We're just smoking some dope together. Child, he gives me free dope." Listen, nothing is free. Yes, the deal is operating, and if it looks like it's too good to be true, then it probably is.

She thinks, "Oh Lord, he's got the best crack. We're just going to smoke this crack together. We're only going to do a line of cocaine." First of all, she already is out of her mind. "We're just gonna do a little cocaine? We're just going to do a couple of lines? Whenever I go over there, I don't have to pay him. He never asks me to sleep with him." No, because he realizes if he can get her high enough, he doesn't have to ask her permission. She won't even remember it tomorrow.

He'll turn her on to drugs, then when her body craves them, has to have them, he'll look at her and say, "Now you're going to have to start working for this. I've been carrying you long enough. Nothing in life is free." Because she's addicted, she'll ask, "Well, what do you want me to do?" She is willing to do whatever it takes to satisfy her craving for drugs. "Well, I have this friend, and he needs a little companionship tonight, about eleven o'clock. If you want some drugs, then you're going to have to do this little appointment for me." There she is, going out there because she thinks it's one time. "I'm going to get my little drugs, and I'm coming on back in." You just opened the door to a new lifestyle, because the more drugs a person consumes, the more they'll need. This man is not going to give her any more free drugs, except to keep her continually addicted to them. Then he will put her out on the street. She will move from just being company to one man to entertaining man after man.

Some of you wondered how people got into prostitution. That's next to the oldest trick in the book, but that's how it works. Man after man after man. Now he has the woman under control; she needs something of which he has control. Her judgment becomes so convoluted by the addiction that she takes the money she made from using her body and brings it to him. She gives him all of it because she knows if she takes some, he'll beat her down. She says that was love? It started out being what she thought was mutually beneficial, but it changed.

Function Before Form: The Key to Partnership

The reason the relationship changed was because she didn't know the thought and the intent of the person's heart when she entered into that relationship. That's why God told Samuel in I Samuel 16:7, "Look not on his countenance . . . ." Don't let the appearance of your friend, or potential friends deceive you. Yes, they may look one way, but in their heart, they may be something else. ". . . or on the height of his stature." Don't let height fool you. Some women say, "I want them tall, dark, and handsome," but your answer may be short, light, and not so attractive. That may be your ticket that will take you on the best ride you've ever had in your life. You don't know where your blessing is, you just know that you like certain physical attributes in a person. The difference between what you like and what you need, as I stated before, is comparable to the distance between the Atlantic and Pacific oceans.

Do you remember the person you fantasized about before you were saved? Recall the type of person you dreamed would be your ideal mate. Look at who you are in a relationship with today. They look nothing alike, I guarantee you. No similarities at all. See, you are attracted to one type of person, but you saw a need for something greater than appearance when you selected your mate. Necessity is not based on looks, although they are wonderful if you can get them. If you can't get the looks, go for the real deal. What good is it to have a car that looks good on the outside but doesn't have an engine? You can park it in front of your house and let grass grow through the floorboard. "Doesn't it look pretty?" Yes, but when are you going to drive it? Look for function. There is a little saying in the architectural arena that I love. I talked to an architect one day and he said, "You know, we have a very basic principle in the school of architectural design: function before form." He said, "A lot of times, because we're humans, we like to get form before function." We're so concerned with how beautiful something is that we build it without questioning its usefulness.

Ask a potential mate or associate, "How are you functioning in your current job?" "How are you functioning with the Lord in prayer?" "How are you functioning with the Lord in your Bible reading and meditation time?" "How is your functionalism with

Him, or do you have a dysfunctional relationship with God?" "Well, if you are dysfunctional with Him, you can't help but be dysfunctional with me. There is no way you love me." If the person says, "Well, I love the Lord," ask, "What's His name?" If the response is God, say, "No, His name is Jesus." (That is the intimate name that only those in true fellowship with Him use.)

All you have to do is ask some basic questions to find out how much they love the Lord and are willing to be led by His spirit. That is what the term "spirit-filled" means. If you introduce the term to the wrong mate, you may receive this response, "Who? That's what I get when I drink my fifth of Vodka." You can tell them, "That is the wrong spirit." "Wine is a mocker, strong drink is raging: and whosoever partaketh is not wise" (Proverbs 20:1). These questions already will have made you aware of their level of commitment to the Lord before you get involved with them. Sometimes one's limited knowledge of God will prevent you from entering into relationship with them.

I have taken a stand, amid criticism, to refuse to marry people with an unsound foundation. Many have become upset and angry, but I have not seen one marriage work out where I declined performing a marriage ceremony. In most cases, these persons will attempt to find someone who is not anointed to watch for their souls (Hebrews 13:7,17) to marry them anyway. In our ministry, couples must submit to four mandatory premarital counseling sessions with myself or another member of our counseling staff. Some become angry because of pressing concerns, but those who go through them have come back after they've been married for some time and say, "Thank you, Pastor."

I also must address the issue of self-esteem. Some individuals base their self-worth on whether they have a mate or not. They run from person to person, begging someone to marry them. "Please marry me. Just give me a chance. Change my name. Just make me yours. If it only lasts two months, it's all right just as long as I can say that I was married one time!" Don't do this because you are wasting yourself away. Have more respect for yourself than this. Always enter relationships believing that a person is getting the deal of a lifetime when they marry you. Yes, you will get a blessing in your spouse, but also believe that your spouse is getting a blessing in you as well. Do not have a one-sided relationship. "Oh, I'll just be so blessed if I have so-and-so." What about them? Are they receiving a blessing too? How do you value yourself?

God tells us not to be persuaded by a person's outward appearance. "Do not look at his countenance, or the height of his stature, because I have refused him." Saul was the best looking thing that Israel had ever seen. A lot of times, looks sway people. In the 1960 presidential election in which Richard Nixon was the Republican candidate running against Democratic candidate John F. Kennedy, America witnessed its first televised presidential debate. Kennedy looked good, young and poised. His answers and responses were well thought out and he was articulate and handsome. However, his opponent, Nixon, was sweating. He had a wart. His hair appeared to be one color on one side, and another color on the other side. Everyone was impressed with the physical appeal of JFK. Immediately after the debate, a consensus was taken and two questions were asked. One was, "If the election was held today, who would you vote for?" Almost hands down, it was JFK. Question two, "Why?" "He was so handsome." What does that have to do with being president?

We are impressed more by the way things look rather than by the way they perform or function. All one has to do is visit a used car lot to see just how moved our society is by external appearances. The owner will have a clunker on the lot, but he will shine it up and put a little tire dressing on the tires. When buyers look at it they think, "It looks like a good car." How can you tell whether it is good or not by the way it looks? You cannot, and dealers know this. They know customers are drawn to the aesthetic appeal of things.

Unlike us, God can see the heart of a matter. He can look behind the scenes of a situation and determine if it will be good or harmful to us. Let's look again at I Samuel 16:7, "Look not on his countenance, or on the height of his stature; because I have refused him: for the Lord seeth not as man seeth . . . ." God sees deeper than we can. He can see things that we cannot. You might have 20/20 vision, but God can see some underlying things your eyes can never tap into. What happens to people in bad relationships is that they'll see problems sooner or later down the road. They may be blind right now, but as they spend time in the relationship, all of a sudden their eyes come open and they see crystal clear. God says that He was seeing that all along. From the beginning, He saw the person was not mutually beneficial.

For some, God has closed the doors to destructive people. You almost married the wrong person five times, and God got them out of your life. Now you're angry at Him, trying to figure out who the sixth person will be. God says, "Okay, I'm going to have to let you go ahead and do it. You're on a collision course with danger, but that's what you prefer."

I'll point out another phenomenon that is occurring—brief engagements. What gets into a person's spirit that causes them to marry an individual they barely know? This trend is sweeping the country, and it is in the body of Christ as well. You know someone for six months, and you want to change your last name. "We're going to get married!" My first question to the couple is, "How long have you known each other?" If they tell me six months, I advise them to see me in a year-and-a-half. I only perform ceremonies that I have received an unction from God that His blessing is upon the union. That way, God's blessing will be upon the marriage, and even if it doesn't work, I'll feel better because I performed the ceremony out of the integrity of my heart.

You see, what looks good to us at that specific moment may not be what God says is good for us in the long run. God can see every angle of a situation the moment we're faced with it, "For the Lord seeth not as a man seeth . . . ." How does a man see, Lord? "Man looketh on the outward appearance, but the Lord looketh on the heart" (I Samuel 16:7). If you want to know who you are in relationship with, it's a matter of the heart, not of outward appearance.

CHAPTER 5

Qualifying Relationships

===================

Now that you have read examples of bridges and burdens, have you been qualifying the people you are involved with? Are you evaluating those in your relationships, whether they are emotional, erotic, or philos (brotherly/sisterly)? You should take time to find out if your involvement is a blessing or a curse. Is it a bridge or is it a burden? Are they helping you or are they hurting you? Are they sharing the load or are they a part of the load? Are you engaged in something that is designed by God or are you in something that either you or Satan constructed? These are powerful questions which will assist in the qualifying process.

If your relationship is too heavy to bear, it is not from God. God will never give you a load that is too heavy to bear (I Corinthians 10:13). Remember the foundational scripture we looked at earlier in this book, "Come unto me, all ye that labor and are heavy laden, and I will give you rest. Take my yoke upon you, and learn of me; for I am meek and lowly in heart: and ye shall find rest unto your souls. For my yoke is easy, and my burden is light" (St. Matthew 11:28-29). God-ordained relationships largely bring a person the ability to rest.

Again, I am qualifying this statement, as I have done all others I've made, by saying that everything I mention regarding relationships is in the ideal sense or the perfect sense. No one person is going to be perfect all of the time. So if you are looking for Mr. or Ms. Right, keep in mind that the individual is not going to be perfect. They are going to have some flaws. Even if you are relating to another individual on a friendly basis, that relationship will have some flaws as well. Largely, however, your significant other should be a bridge. Most of the time this person should be helping you, aiding you, not slowing you down. If you are in any kind of relationship at all, and the majority of the time it is causing a hindrance, a blockade, or it is causing you to be hampered from accomplishing things, then you probably need to seek God about how and when to move on.

The Christian Example

While we are talking about relationships, we also need to keep in mind that Christians have to be a picture to the world of how people should get along and progress. The world should be able to look at the body of Christ and see how they are supposed to interact with each other. If they look at us and cannot see an example, then how are they going to have any idea of how the process should work? In contrast to the world, Jesus taught that we are the "light of the world" (St. Matthew 5:14). The world is supposed to look inside the walls of the church and see light (correct information). Jesus also said that we are the "salt of the earth." You are the best thing this earth has to offer. You are the greatest thing this earth has going for it. If Jesus returned and removed Christians from the earth, the planet would disassemble. It would become very wicked. As a matter of fact, the Tribulation cannot even take place as long as those who have accepted Jesus Christ are in the earth. God has to rapture us in order for the earth to become irreversibly evil and corrupt. With the body of believers being here as the light of the world—while delaying the tribulation—we are supposed to give the world a picture of how relationships should operate. We should show them how to make the appropriate selection of people to fulfill the critical roles of our lives and how to avoid choosing the first person who comes along, unless sufficient proof indicates God sent them.

The world should see that the Christian community has the love of God effervescing in our presence. The Bible says the love of God constrains us (II Corinthians 5:14). We should walk in love more than anyone in the world, in the universe. That's relationship. I'm supporting you, and you're supporting me. That's good Biblical relationship.

One thing Christians must learn in order to get along with each other in church relationships is that we are very different in many cases. Men differ from women, and women differ from men. Because of the way we're built emotionally, at times, trivial things can immensely upset us that really do not have to. Little things, such as someone sitting by your spouse. Husbands may become upset if the wrong type of man sits beside their wife too many times in church services. Wives, the wrong type of woman can sit beside your husband too often and you'll become upset as well. This should not be the case in the Christian family.

Let's also keep in mind that we have to play by good, fair rules. Husbands and wives, you do have grounds to be upset in certain situations. If someone is plotting to attract the attention of your husband or your wife and keeps sitting by them, I would be watchful too. It can be upsetting to know someone is attempting to attract someone else's spouse. One of the basic laws of nature is to protect what is yours. Some women have mastered this law. I say they are "hawks." They sit high on perches and look low to see everything. They see it before it becomes a reality. They see it in the "spirit." Women say to me, "I saw it in the spirit." In my mind, I say, "I understand. . .the spirit of jealousy, ha ha."

The second thing Christians must be mindful of is our display of affection. We are very loving people, but we must be watchful how we display our love towards each other. For example, how we greet and hug fellow believers. I'm extremely tall, so I don't have a real big problem. However, average-height men run into problems hugging women exactly their height. Some time ago while very young in ministry experience, I remember I had just finished ministering and a lady who had recently lost someone in her family came up to me. I was tired and perspiring and had an overcoat on. I was not alert, and I was ready to go home. The lady came into the church and was telling me about the situation, and she started crying. I was so concerned with her being distraught that I didn't see her next action coming. Most of the time I know how to position people so they don't embrace me with improper contact, but she approached me so quickly that I didn't have a chance to move myself around to avoid an uncomfortable and otherwise question-able stance. She ran into the church and grabbed me. She gave me a full body contact hug. I mean, you could have dropped a dime in between us and couldn't have found it for five minutes. She had a wrestling hold on me. She gripped me. I was much smaller then, but she had a big hold on me! This woman wasn't desirable to me; she wasn't my type. She was nothing I would want or liked, but she was a woman. My body wasn't asking any questions about how she looked, whether she was desirable or whether she was my type. My body said one thing, "This is a woman, and she is *too* close!"

I derived from that experience that there is such a thing as a "holy" hug and an "unholy" hug. If you are a woman, you do not want to give an unholy hug to a man because whether his spirit has just left the altar of heaven or not, he is still in a flesh robe. If you are a woman, this is how you should hug: put the shoulder on him. If a man says to you, "Hold on, I want to give you a big hug," place your shoulder into his chest.

Also, women, you have to learn how to hug if you wear a lot of makeup. Put your hand on a man's shoulder so that you lean your face on your hand. You will avoid putting your face print on his clothing. I'm talking about relationships, good relationships. Let's examine this issue in I Peter 5:14: "Greet ye one another with a kiss of charity" (The King James Bible). "Salute one another with a kiss of love [the symbol of mutual affection]" (The Amplified Bible).

The kiss and the hug of charity is not the kiss and the hug of lust or desire. There is a difference. The scripture is not referring to erotic love, but brotherly/sisterly love. You should hug your broth-ers and sisters in church just like you hug your biological siblings.

Sure, there will be someone in your church who you find attrac-tive. Sometimes you will need to mix it up and avoid sitting beside the same person during every service. Don't give the enemy an opportunity. If you're sitting beside the same person who is lighting your fire, and you're trying to listen to your pastor's teaching but the enemy is talking to you, sit beside someone that you do not find attractive and let your love gift begin to make room for you.

On another note, some people have to treat their spouse better at home so they won't be tempted to pursue someone else at church who they feel will appreciate them more. Some people are so mean at home that their spouse is looking for someone to be nice to them, and church is a good place for that to happen. You're mean and won't talk, but your mate desires someone who is kind and will converse.

Unity: The Key to Healthy Relationships

Let's look at another aspect of Godly relationships—unity. Ecclesiastes 4:9 says, "Two are better than one; because they have a good (more satisfying) reward for their labor. For if they fall, the one will lift up his fellow." Solomon is not saying everyone has to be in a marital relationship. He is saying that all of us need people in our lives to fulfill some function we could not complete alone. It has good reward; it has good benefit; it has a good point of destination to it. It is a bridge if you have the right person in your life. Others can help prevent failure. Here, Solomon is talking about unity; where one goes, the other is willing to follow. If one is in the ditch, the other acts as a point of leverage where they can raise their partner up.

If you are with someone, you have a vested interest. That is what relationship is about. Relationships are about giving and receiving, so there is a vested interest. I am interested in you because you have invested into my life, and you are interested in me because I have invested into your life as well. You may discover you are in relationships with people you cannot get out of because you have contributed too much into them. Marriage, for instance, is too much of an investment for divorce to take place. My wife told me once, "If you leave me, you must be out of your mind. Find a rich woman, because you're going to have to live on $70 a week."—I am not going anywhere!

Also, do not get into a relationship with people if you are not willing to be with them when they fall. The test of a good relationship is not how faithful you are when everything is going fine. The truth of the matter is, you don't really need people that much when everything is going well for you. When trouble is in your life and you are going through a test and trial, that is when you really need someone. I tell people all the time not to progress from the dating stage to the marital stage until you have allowed the individual to be tested through trouble. Find out how they are going to respond to you when you are in trouble. For example, when you have no money; when your health is challenged; when you've lost a job; when you're discouraged; when you're going through those changes in life, see how the person you're dating responds to you. You will know whether they will be a good mate for life. Ask yourself, "Is this the person whom I want with me when I have to bury my parent(s) or when facing some other form of grief? Can they provide comfort to me when I am feeling alone or discouraged?"

". . . woe to him that is alone when he falleth . . . ."
—Ecclesiastes 4:10

Let's read the remainder of the scripture in Ecclesiastes, ". . . but woe to him that is alone when he falleth; for he hath not another to help him up." Now this goes beyond the obvious impression of the scripture. I believe King Solomon was saying that it is a disadvantage to a person who thinks they are in a good relationship until they fall and find out the person they thought they could count on is really unreliable. The word "woe" means deep sorrow or grief, misfortune, calamity, or dismay.

I have counseled often, and I have found that there are many devastated people in marriages. They thought their spouse was going to be a certain way for life, but their spouse changed. Their spouse didn't prove to be what they needed them to be in a time of need. It's devastating. Have you ever been let down by someone? Multiply that feeling by a lifetime. When you are married to a relationship of any type and your spouse (or whoever you are counting on) is constantly letting you down, you can't count on them for anything. It's sad. You shouldn't have someone in your life who is supposed to help you, yet you still end up doing everything by yourself. Two are supposed to be better than one, not worse and not the same. If you are in a relationship, let your partner know you love him or her by doing something. Accept your responsibility. If you are supposed to be a bridge, you have to carry your load.

Think about these questions: Why are you in a relationship? What do you want to get out of it that you cannot receive being by yourself? When your reasons are right for wanting to be in a relationship or partnership, your outcome stands a really good chance of being successful.

The Bible emphasizes that relationships have been designed to provide help. Ecclesiastes 4:11 says, "Again, if two lie together, they have heat." How many of you understand this principle? If you are in trouble and you have someone else with you, it is a better feeling. If you have someone by your side encouraging and believing in you, you'll begin to believe that you can come out of any situation. You have the heat that represents creativity. If you are going through trouble, seek God to place someone in your life who can give you inspiration. If it's cold (empty) in your life, you need heat.

Some people are going through a great deal of emotional and psychological distresses. Do you know the No. 1 thing Satan tries to get them to do? He encourages them to be alone all of the time. That is the worst thing they can do. Satan then has them on neutral ground where he can bombard their minds. He will tell them about suicide. He will give them a good case of depression. He'll tell them to take themselves out, nobody cares. "Look, you haven't had a date since Nixon resigned." He'll just keep going on and on. They'll become more and more depressed until they begin to consume alcohol, and once they begin drinking, they won't be able to think correctly. Then they'll call up someone who used to like them and if they can't get them to come by, they'll become further depressed. They start browsing through photo albums, admiring their younger pictures, and comparing them to how they look now. They become more depressed until after a while, suicide sounds like a good idea.

If you are going through changes, stay connected to a Bible-teaching, faith-in-action, word church! You should be there all of the time because you will have heat! I'm not talking about natural heat; I'm referring to spiritual heat. The illumination comes from God's Word to let you know that He "will never leave thee, nor forsake thee" (Hebrews 13:5). You have to understand that you are not in your situation by yourself. There is nothing like going through trouble in your life and having someone in your corner telling you, "Hey, it's not over, you can come out. It's not that bad. We're going to make it out of this thing." When you have that encouragement, you can conquer the world! Glory to God in heaven!

Ecclesiastes Chapter 4 continues, ". . . but how can one be warm alone?" How can he have inspiration? How can he have revelation? How can he have information—alone? God desires humans to interact with one another to keep each other hearing uplifting words that will enable us to progress supernaturally.

Having the person God has ordained to be in your life also will assist you in spiritual warfare. Instead of facing the enemy alone, you'll have someone else who is backing you up. Ecclesiastes 4:12 states, "And if one prevails against him, two shall withstand him." You should write over that phrase, "Satan." If Satan tries to fight you, two of you can withstand him. That is, you have a brother or sister walking in agreement with you.

Jesus says in St. Matthew 18:18, "Whatsoever ye shall bind on earth shall be bound in heaven: and whatsoever ye shall loose on earth shall be loosed in heaven." He also says in Verse 19, "That if two of you shall agree on earth as touching anything that they shall ask, it shall be done." Agreement is a state of mind. It is an attitude of acknowledging and accepting the mind-set, word, or opinion of another. Agree in the spirit that what the Word of God says is true. When you have this kind of agreement, the only thing you'll need to do when trouble comes is continue saying what the Word has said. Also, when your partner agrees with you, they are saying they'll be there with you through tests and trials, telling you what the Word says. Jesus says if people get into that mode, they will have whatever they ask of the Father.

Some of us simply need to have a person or persons in our lives—from a Christian perspective—to tell us when we get "off-key." We ask for a lot of things that aren't even in the Word of God. If it's not in the Word of God, you don't have any right to ask for it. It's not good for you. Everything you need that is good for you is in the Bible. (St. Matthew 7:7-11) All the promises in Christ Jesus are yes and amen. (II Corinthians 1:20) God has given us all things that pertain to life and godliness. (II Peter 1:3) Everything you need is in the Bible. Don't just ask out of selfish emotion.

Even when it comes to choosing a mate, employee, friend, or business partner, don't allow your emotions to decide for you. Seek someone who you are spiritually compatible with. If I were a Christian looking for someone to partner with, I would not talk to people who aren't saved. What in the world can they possibly do for you? If they unite with you, they must love Jesus. You may say, "Well, I like the way they look." Forget looks! That person is a son or daughter of the devil! They should be moving toward Jesus. If they do receive salvation, watch them for a while and make sure they didn't just get saved for you to connect with them. I have been in ministry long enough to know that does not last. If they got saved to get you, then when they become tired of you, all they have to do is backslide. They know if salvation was your prerequisite, all they have to do is walk away from it, and you'll leave. Keep in mind that in between the time they cut covenant with you and break up with you, they have access to your emotional goods. Seek God to be in a relationship with people who are saved and on equal footing with you spiritually.

A person's strength lies in the number of people supporting them. "And if one (Satan) prevails against him, two shall withstand him; and a threefold cord is not quickly broken" (Ecclesiastes 4:12). This threefold cord represents the trinity of God. God is in relationship with the Son and the Holy Spirit. They are all intermingled in relationship. Just as they trust and depend on themselves, you must make trust and reliability important as well.

Show Yourself Friendly

I am a little cautious of people who are not in relationship with anyone. They have no friends and they don't like people. I realize there are times when you want to be alone. My wife will tell you that at times I don't want to see people because I need the Lord to speak to me alone. There are times when I don't want anyone to call my name. I need to be alone sometimes. When I am finished being by myself, however, I want people around me.

What concerns me is people who never, ever, want anyone around them. Have you decided to have great friends? The wiser you become, the more you should desire to have them. You begin to learn that life is not about things as much as it's about people. If you have great friends, you can have a great life! At times, I get so much enjoyment sitting around and entertaining all afternoon and into the night. I'll be tired that night, but I get up feeling good because I've been refreshed by people. That is one of the basic needs of human existence, the need for human companionship. If you want people to surround you, then you have to be worthy of people. People should enjoy being around you. If you are mean, hateful, backstabbing, malicious, conniving, maniacal, and diabolical (need I go further?), not too many people will want to be around you. Solomon, the writer of the book of Proverbs, says he that has friends must first take step one, "show himself friendly" (Proverbs 18:24).

Some people do not pass the friendly test at church. Church is a great testing ground because it is a dichotomy of the world and it is Christ's body. If you cannot get along with people there, you will not be ready to go to the world. Some people have been in a church for three years and still do not know anyone. That may be a reason why they don't have any friends. If you cannot meet people at church—a friendly church where people are reaching out to you—then what are you going to do in the world? People speak to you and you turn your head in the opposite direction. You have iceberg feelings and do not make eye-to-eye contact with people, as if someone is going to rob you. People pass by you in church and you clutch your purse or grip your wallet pocket for security.

Open yourself up! Yes, you might have been hurt before, but the chances are good that people in your local church did not hurt you. You can't resign and say, "I'm not going to give other people a chance." The last person you were involved with may have hurt you, but the one you've been avoiding might bless you. You close opportunities when you close the doors to relationships.

God-Ordained Relationships Will Help You Cross Over

As I stated before, God-ordained relationships always will be a bridge. They will lead you to cross over. They will not be burdensome to you. God will place individuals in your life to help you cross over. There may be some things you'll have to deal with in the relationship, but the overall aspect will be in the direction of crossing over. If every person will be honest, they will admit that we all have things we need to get over. Will you also agree that some things you will not get over unless you have human help?

I think of how amazing it has been to watch my oldest son grow from a boy who was very good in school both academically and socially, and not interested a whole lot in the opposite gender, to a young man who now realizes that a woman can be a gift from God. While it is amazing to me, every young man and young woman experiences this as they transition into adulthood.

As this process begins, parents actually can see their children change. They are more outgoing and they are concerned about what the opposite gender thinks. It's a major concern. My son may iron and change outfits three times before he leaves the house. I like that. It tells me he wants to look good when he walks out the door. He may change his shoes and then ask me, "Dad, what do you think about these shoes and pants?" I remember what seems like a few days ago, it wouldn't have mattered. His outfit may not have even matched. He may have had on a brown shoe and a black shoe and he would have left home with the mind-set, "They're shoes, aren't they?" He cares about his appearance now. From that perspective, it is also the same thing when we begin to look at the relationships God gives us.

Your "Gift" Will Make Room for You

In Proverbs 18:16 we read, "A man's gift makes room for him, and brings him before great men." When God begins to bestow certain things into your life, those things will make room for you. What am I saying? I am saying because my son is more concerned now about his appearance, in a lot of respects, they make room for him in the broader area where he wants to be included. When God begins to place certain gifts into your life, it makes room for you and brings you before great people. You never have to spend all of your creative energies thinking about attracting someone. So many Christians waste a lot of time doing this. Let me say this before I give a revelatory truth: if you want to get someone, you must become "get-worthy." If you want a rich man, please know that a rich man usually wants a rich woman. If you desire a rich woman, she customarily will desire a wealthy reciprocal. There are exceptions to the rule, but they are very few. Some men say, "I want a queen for a wife. I want a woman that 'ain't' never had 'no' children." But they have 10 in separate places themselves. "I want a virgin." And you do not even know where the letter "V" is located in the alphabet, sexually speaking. I hear crazy talk like this in the body of Christ, but you must be realistic with yourself.

I have met women who say, "I want a man," but every time they leave home they look like a recycling center, a collecting bin where old phone books and newspapers are thrown. You don't want a man. You couldn't be serious. By the same token, I hear men say, "I want a woman, I want a good Christian woman." Yet they don't even know where a Bible is. Your gift is going to make room for you. It will make room with a great woman. It will make room with a great man, a great employer, a great employee, great friends. As a matter of fact, if you get this principle it will make great room before a great number of people. I believe Christians should have an abundance of everything. Jesus said in St. John 10:10, " . . . I am come that they might have life, and that they might have it more abundantly." If you are a woman who desires to be married, you should have an abundance of men waiting at your doorstep, because you have the anointing of God in you. In this application of Proverbs 18:16, your "gift" or what you know makes room for you. I ask people, "What do you have to offer? What are you going to do with a man when he is ready to eat?" Some responses I receive are, "We're going out." Every man loves to go out, but after a while he gets tired of eating in restaurants. He wants something home-cooked. A woman once told me, "Well, one thing about my husband, if I ever get one, he's going to have very white teeth." I said, "Why?" She replied, " 'Cause he's going to eat a lot of ice cream and drink a lot of milk." I told her, "No, you're not going to get a man; you may attract a cat, but not a man." If she attracts a man, he will not stay for very long. He will go next door to a woman who can cook. He'll ease out of her house, drinking her milk, and walk next door to get something to eat! The lady next door might be opening her door, fanning the aroma of food in his direction. He knows he doesn't get good food at home, and if he stays next door too long, he may never return.

You need to have a gift to make that particular kind of room for you. What do you have to offer to the relationship? If you say, "I'm nice." Okay, what else? That alone is not enough of a gift to make the necessary or desired room. In this society, everything is competitive and you need additional attributes to give you the competitive edge. This is what is meant when the scripture says "It makes room for you." I see people all the time who have the wrong philosophy. All one has to do is look at the videos of secular musical artists. One person may be able to sing well, but so can the 100 other artists who are out there making hits. That's serious competition. You need something that is going to cause you to rise and excel that number and make room for you. Although secularly they may use it to gratify Satan, that something is called the gift of God or the anointing of God.

The anointing of God will lead you to be a bridge when everyone else is a burden. As a matter of fact, you may be horrible to look at physically, but if you have an anointing on you, someone will make the extra effort required to see you. Brother, you may be as undesirable as two left shoes, but if you have the anointing of God on you, the gift will make room. It will then help you groom yourself better. The anointing will help you do the best you can with what you have. Grooming is very important. It also is important to know that not everyone will live on "High Fashion Avenue." Not everyone will be stellar in their appearance. You should do the best you can with what you already have. Parents used to teach that if you don't have much, at least take what you do have and make it look the best that you can. After feeding on God's word and attending Bible teaching and training church for a while, you are supposed to be getting yourself together.

The Destructive Nature of a Burden
(Reducing Your Bridge to a Burden)

Let's look at another passage of scripture that will help us identify bridges and burdens. I'm going to use Genesis 3:1 to show you what happens when man has a relationship with each of these two classes of people. What we should be seeking to do is to get all of our relationships either on one column or the other. Either all of them are bridges, or if you are psychotic, all of them are burdens. Your list should evolve to include all of one or all of the other. Either dissolve the heavy ones or develop them into lighter ones, because if you have one that is a bridge and another that's a burden, after a while the burden is going to pull on the bridge.

> "Now the serpent was more subtle than any beast of the field which the Lord God had made. And he said unto the woman, 'Yea, hath God said, Ye shall not eat of every tree of the garden?' And the woman said unto the serpent, 'We may eat of the fruit of the trees of the garden: but of the fruit of the tree which is in the midst of the garden, God has said, Ye shall not eat of it, neither shall ye touch it, lest ye die.' And the serpent said to the woman, 'Ye shall not surely die . . . .'"

Satan is a burden, and anyone in your life who questions the validity and authority of the Word of God is a burden to you. They may not be one today, but they will be by tomorrow. If they are always trying to persuade you away from your standard of holiness or standards of the Word of God, then they are going to be a burden to you. If they tell you, "You know, God didn't mean all that." Burden! "Why do you have to go to church all the time?" Burden! "Why are you giving tithes?" Burden! "The Lord doesn't want you to live right all of the time. He gave you those feelings." Burden!!!

Eve didn't realize this in Satan. In Verses 5 and 6, she allows the burden to continue talking to her. "For God doth know that in the day ye eat thereof, then your eyes shall be opened, and ye shall be as gods, knowing good and evil. And the woman saw the tree was good for food."

God never told Eve the tree would not be good for food; he just told her not to eat of it. The burden is going to lead you to a lot of things that are going to be good for what it is designed for, but it won't be good for your overall relationship. The fruit was good for the nourishment, but it was not good for her relationship with her husband and with God. Begin to look for someone who will benefit you overall. Don't look for a person who will benefit your body, but take away from your earnings and emotions. In Verse 6, Eve makes a bad decision based on the way the fruit looked, "and that it was pleasant to the eyes . . . ." Everything the burden tells you is not going to be unattractive. Satan knows that he has to make things attractive to you, or else you will not accept it. Now that does not mean you should do your best to be unattractive. The remainder of Verse 6 shows how dangerous it was for Eve to talk to a burden, ". . . and a tree to be desired to make one wise, she took of the fruit thereof, and did eat, and gave also unto her husband with her; and he did eat."

Now she was supposed to be a bridge to the man! Because she constantly is talking to a burden, however, she evolves into a burden. Some people are a bridge, bless God. God has saved you and delivered you. He has given you a good head on your shoulders, but now you begin to consistently talk to people who do not have good sense, who have not come into the knowledge of God. They begin to infiltrate your mind with their ungodly thinking, and now the ordained bridge evolves into a burden. There is one devastating thing about a burden: once it becomes one, it burdens everything involved with it.

CHAPTER 6

Letting Go of Destructive Relationships

===

Earlier in this book, we looked at the word "relationship," and I said it can be defined as a personal connection with another by blood, marriage, sexual intercourse, association, etc. We've discovered that God-given relationships are a bridge the vast majority of the time. If God has in fact sent an individual into your life, he or she was sent to be a bridge to help you pass over to the next level. If your load is just as heavy as it otherwise would have been without them being present, or if it is heavier, then guess what? You do not have a blessing, you have a curse.

God did not place a single person in your life to make your way hard. Some people are, unfortunately, drawn to those who make their lives difficult. They'll hold on to them and almost lose their life, all in the name of love and relationship. Some women who have been physically abused have told me they remain in those relationships because they are still in love with the man who is the source of their abuse. Men are the same way. I have asked some of whom I've pastored, "Well brother, why are you still holding on?" They say, "Man, I just love that woman." And I tell them, "Okay, that's wonderful. That was nice when you were 16, but you're older now. Move on." Look at things and determine if they are a bridge or a burden. Deal with them this way.

I also have seen the person who will blame their partner for the trouble in their relationship. They'll look at their partner and say, "You know what? You're a burden to me." Yet when I counsel with them, I find both are burdening each another. If you are in a relationship with a burden, it is probably true that you are a burden as well. Likes attract. Do not put the other person down, saying, "You're not this, you're not that," or "You don't do this, you don't do that." When you turn the situation around, the same shoe probably fits your foot as well. This piece of advice is for those of you who are unequally yoked, or those who are about to enter into a relationship, but are not sure how to evaluate the other person to see if they are qualified to be with you. People should have to be qualified to be in a relationship with you. Everyone can't be your friend. You shouldn't just marry anybody. The persons who find themselves drawn to you should have to qualify to be in your life.

David's Relationship with God: The Perfect Example of a Bridge

In the previous section of this book, we compared bridges and burdens from the scriptures. Now let's look at David and his relationship with God as a perfect example of a bridge. All of us should look into our circle of friends, acquaintances, and people of influence—positively and negatively—to see if they are bridges or burdens. We have a clear-cut example in I Samuel 16:1-12 of how a good, healthy relationship should work.

"And the Lord said unto Samuel, 'How long wilt thou mourn for Saul, seeing I have rejected him from reigning over Israel? Fill thine horn with oil, and go, I will send thee to Jesse the Bethlehemite: for I have provided me a king among his sons.'"

Before I continue, I would like for you to keep in mind that there may come a time in your life when you may have to move on from certain relationships. Have you ever seen people who want to hold on to a certain friend? They want to hold on to an old love affair. They do not want to let a relationship go. Sometimes it's already gone and they need only to wake up and realize it.

The prophet Samuel was like one of those people. He was still holding on to his past relationship with the current king, Saul. Samuel loved Saul and thought surely God should have been able to do something with him, but God told Samuel to move on. In other words, He said, "Sammy, Sam, my friend, my son, my servant, Saul no longer is going to qualify to be a bridge. He now has become a burden, and the only thing you can do with him is move on."

Steer Clear of Goats and Hirelings

We'll return to this scripture in a moment, but now let's read St. John 10:11. Jesus says, "I am the good shepherd: the good shepherd giveth his life for the sheep." The good shepherd (bridge) will not give his life for a goat (burden), yet some Christians are doing this very thing. God did not tell us to concern ourselves with that animal. He has horns and he'll take you out! Not only that, but goats are destructive—they'll eat up everything. Neither do they restore nor replace anything they've destroyed. They devour all you let them get to. Some of you are thinking now. Your biographical list is going through your mind. You're probably thinking about people and putting the name "goat" over their pictures. You're seeing them for who they are. As a goat, they take from you and never restore anything. Jesus said the good shepherd will only give, and he'll give his life for a sheep.

Continue reading Verse 12, "But he that is an hireling, and not the shepherd, whose own the sheep are not, seeth the wolf coming, and leaveth the sheep, and fleeth: and the wolf catcheth them, and scattereth the sheep. The hireling fleeth, because he is an hireling, and careth not for the sheep." A hireling, or a hired servant, is not in relationship with you because they love you. They are burdens who are in it for personal benefit. Some people attach themselves to you because of what you have. Others do so because of who you are, where you've been, where you live, or what you drive. All of these things are good to have in your life, but they aren't a sound basis to build a relationship upon. When these commodities run out, the hired person is going to leave. They'll figure, "There's nothing to pay me with. I came here looking for a payment." If, however, a person really loves you for who you are, they will be there with you, even if you don't have anything. As a matter of fact, they will help you acquire possessions.

A hireling also will attempt to come into your life, at any facet, without making a commitment. They are not interested in ownership; they want to lease or rent, making payments as they can. They contribute to you and your vision very infrequently, like seeing you the first of the month, an installment plan of sorts. I say again, there is a major difference between a man who rents a house and one who purchases a home. A renter knows it's not his house, so if something is damaged, he's thinking, "It's not mine." Something else can get broken and he'll think, "I don't care, it's not mine." He may not cut the grass. Why? "Not mine!" Anyone who will subject themselves to being merely rented does not understand that the other person does not have their best interests at heart. They don't care.

I have rented and I have owned some things, and I know there is a difference. While I was in college, I rented a house that I loved and kept up, but in the back of my mind I knew it was not my house. For instance, I told the landlord there was a leak in the faucet. He took his own time getting around to repair it, so I expressed my discontentment to him. I told him, "It can rot the wood if it wants to, I'll just move." You see, when people enter into relationship with you, if they haven't really bought into you, they have not purchased you, so to speak. They haven't come into your life under a God-given commandment, a God-given agreement, so when things go wrong, they easily can move on. You can hold an armful of feelings for them, but if God did not place them in your life, they will walk on those feelings. However, if God did place them in your life, they may not agree with you and they may dislike what's going on at the time, but they will be there. You can count on them even through disagreements. You can sit down and reason with them and they won't laugh at you. The Word says that there is a friend who sticks closer than a brother (Proverbs 18:24). Now that's a good relationship.

A hireling is the worst person to have guarding your belongings, or anything in your life that is of any value, especially during the threat of trouble. For when he "seeth the wolf coming, (he) leaveth the sheep, and fleeth." Have you had this happen? I remember being a young man in school, and learning something my parents didn't teach me. I learned it from a classmate who dated a couple of women at the same time, but he never let them find out about each other. He always managed to get into an argument with them before Valentine's Day and Christmas. That way he wouldn't have to buy them any gifts. He'd get into an argument for no reason, slam the phone down, and act as if he was totally out of the relationship until after the holidays passed. Then all of a sudden, he'd remember their phone numbers and call them up again saying, "I'm sorry. I'm so sorry." He saw the "wolf" coming. The wolf in this case was Valentine's Day and Christmas, something that would challenge his resolve, and when he saw the wolf coming, he left the sheep, thus defining him as a hireling.

Women, in many instances, become involved with an average looking man who treats them well, yet they leave this good man when a more handsome one comes their way. The one they're dating has a lot of good qualities. He pays the rent, buys the comb that combs their hair, so to speak. Then, all of a sudden, someone else who looks better shows up and they walk away from their good thing. They see a wolf coming and prefer to romance him. All women do not like nice men. Some are attracted to evil guys because they find them exciting. They get a rush from their life-styles. If God, however, did not arrange that relationship, the hireling will abandon them. God has not made us to be abandoned. He doesn't like to see you cast aside. Remember Adam? God looked at him and said, "It is not good for man to be alone" (Genesis 2:18). When you are by yourself, Satan attacks. You are a prime target for the enemy. He can inundate your mind. He attempts to come in and sell you a bad bill of goods. God says, "I don't want you by yourself. I always want to be able to place other people in your life who can be a blessing, or a bridge to help you cross over."

The hireling leaves the sheep, and fleeth, and the wolf catches the sheep and scattereth them. The hireling fleeth because he is a hireling; he doesn't have the mind-set of the owner. Jesus is not trying to get into relationship with the hireling, the wolf, or the goat, because of their nature. The only relationship you can have with anyone who is not a sheep is one that gets them born again, so they can change their nature. If you're involved with sinners (who perpetuate sin because that is what "sinners" do), understand that they are not born-again. They do not possess God's nature inside of them. Regardless of the type of relationship, whether you're involved with a sinner in a friendship, dating, business, or marital setting, it is unavoidable for this person to produce after the nature of the one they are associated with. The one they're associated with is their father, the devil (St. John 8:44). Watch people before taking them in too closely. Determine if they live a saved (set apart for God's usage) lifestyle for a period of time. If you do not take these precautions, the effects can be damaging and very devastating.

Don't be Afraid to Let Go

Many people find it difficult to let a bad relationship go. Samuel was dealing with this when God ended his relationship with Saul. In I Samuel 16:1, God said to Samuel, "How long will you mourn for Saul, seeing I have rejected him from reigning over Israel . . .?" How long have you been mourning over a dead relationship? You are holding onto things in the spirit of your mind that will never work. One simple principle to bear in mind is this: if God says something won't work, then it won't work. There is no use in trying to get involved in it to see. Satan is into sin, and it would be hard for you to beat him at the game he invented. He is the master of it. In many cases, we flirt with sin thinking we see a way to come out of it unaffected. We fail to realize that he mastered and engineered the game of sin; he has some crooks in it we don't know about.

Samuel was being asked if he would continue dealing with something God had already said would not work. I have put this to the test. When you are born-again and filled with the Spirit; and you meet people, almost instantaneously you know whether you should include them in your circle of friends or reject them. You have the barometer of truth and peace inside of you now. I can meet people, and when they walk through the door, instantly I know whether it is a person I want to seek further relationship with or someone who I'll never have another conversation with. I don't have to pray about it, I already know. When God gives you the barometer on the inside of you to dispense and measure out the truth, and He says something won't work, pack your grip because it's over. If you try to make it work in disobedience to God's instructions, you will suffer.

I remember praying about this matter and God said to me, "There are many people who become so desperate about marriage, that they will go outside the body of Christ and marry a sinner." He continued, "I told them from the beginning that it will not work." The only thing you can do, my precious sister, my precious brother, when you get into a situation like this is to tolerate it and pray for your partner. That is all you can do. The individual, the goat, the wolf, the hireling, will hurt you. That is all they can do because they are of their father, the devil, and his works are what they do (St. John 8:44).

If you are honest with yourself, you will agree that the only response to this hurt is to tolerate it or move on. In some situations, you may have to pray and get the sensitivity of God. He may tell you to stay in the relationship and tough it out. In other situations, it may be time to move on, but you will have to seek God for the answer for your life.

When God has rejected someone from being in a certain position, honor His decision. His plan is to keep you from suffering loss at the hand of the enemy. You may be reluctant just as Samuel was, but you'll have a better life on the other side of your obedience to God. He'll speak to you just as He spoke to Samuel. God said to him, "I've rejected him from reigning over Israel. Fill your horn with oil." In other words, pack your Louis Vuitton and split! You are not going to lose anything if nothing is there.

I knew a minister once who made his living by taking advantage of believers. He and his wife were a very lazy couple who traveled from house to house with their children, freeloading off people who felt sorry for them. I watched that couple for a long time bring a bad name on God. Then one day, I had a chance to confront the husband. He asked me for assistance, and when I didn't agree to help him, he tried to project a guilt complex on me. So I asked to see him at a later time. I told him exactly what I had observed. I said, "You're lazy and your wife is lazy. The only reason I would ever bless you is because of your children that you brought into this world, who didn't ask to come here. As for you and your wife, I could see you starving in the street, and wouldn't do a cotton-picking thing about it." They didn't have a church or anyone sponsoring them because they would not commit anywhere consistently. He thought that since he preached well, it was the saints' responsibility to support him and his family. They would go to a believer's house to visit, then he would say, "The Lord told me to stay here." It might be a month before the Lord told him to move on!

What you have to understand is that God has not placed anyone in your life to deplete you, to sponge off you. One Christian lady and her husband had compassion on the family. She told me that although her husband was not saved, he was a nice man, so he let them come into their house. I could not believe it. This man was a sinner, but since he stayed under the influence of alcohol most of the time, he probably didn't realize what was going on. She said, "Let me tell you what happened to me when I took those folks into my house. I was going to work every day, and when I left the house, they would still be in the bed. By midday, they would get up." She had steaks in the freezer about an inch to an inch-and-a-half thick. She said. "They'd fry those for breakfast." I said to her, "Oh No! The mother, the father, and her children, would be out of my house." She also told me that she would buy soft drinks by the case and that family would drink them up in one day. She thought they were going to change and was trying to be in relationship with them. Listen, if a person is a sponge, this is what they are, and they can't do anything but absorb. When this lady threw that family out of her house, she felt guilty for a long time. I told her, "Sister, you did the right thing, believe me."

God will not ordain people to come into your life to take advantage of you, as in the case of Saul. As soon as God told Samuel to leave relationship with him, He said, "Fill your horn with oil and go, and I will send thee to Jesse the Bethlehemite, for I have provided me a king among his sons." The Spirit revealed this to me: God provided a *new* king. God may be moving you to a new place, to a new family, to a new relationship, to a new job. Let me tell you something, precious ones, God will tell you to do something that will move you to a higher position in life. He'll tell you, "You've been on that job long enough, I'm going to move you."

I have found that it is difficult for people to leave something they've been attached to. They will hold on to a $5.50 an hour job that they've had for 20 years. If someone says a company is hiring elsewhere at $13.30 an hour, they'll say, "I don't know. I heard over there . . . ." Well, whatever they are going through over there for an additional $7.80 an hour could be better for you overall if you take it. Sometimes the Lord will say, "Go, I've already prepared another way." You will never see another way until you go.

If people threaten to leave you, tell them to go. They are probably in the way. Tell them, "Somebody else is watching me, go!" There are even times when people are ready to go to be with the Lord, but their loved ones want to keep them on this side of life. They are saved, 93 years old, and have a $200,000 life insurance policy, and they're ready to go. But you pray, "Lord, keep them here." If you haven't paid your mortgage in five months, and they have a $200,000 policy (of which you are the beneficiary) and are ready to go, let them go. They no longer want to live, they have money for you, and God is calling them. Many of us hold on. We hold on to things and choke the growth that God would give us.

When it comes to separating from a person you've been in relationship with for some time, some people share the feeling Samuel had in Verse 2, "If Saul hears it, he will kill me." I've counseled people with this same fear. "My boyfriend will take me out." Honey, if he has that mentality, then he has taken you out already. You are not losing a thing. Some people get excited about this sick kind of love. "If I can't have you, nobody else can." Whenever a person tells you that, leave! Find the quickest exit door, because that is a psychotic person.

Samuel was afraid of Saul's reaction, so the Lord gave him specific instructions that would guarantee protection from any harm Saul might have tried to cause him. In Verses 3 and 4, the Lord said, "Take an heifer with thee, and say, 'I am come to sacrifice to the Lord.'" In other words, if you do what I tell you, no harm can come to you. There is protection in obedience. When you obey God as it relates to your relationships, there is protection in it. Let's continue. "And call Jesse to the sacrifice, and I will shew thee what thou shalt do: and thou shalt anoint unto me him whom I name unto thee. And Samuel did that which the Lord spake . . . ."

Samuel did exactly what the Lord told him. He went to Bethlehem. Some of you need a change of vicinity. If you keep catching the same kind of fish, that is probably the only kind in that lake. Go to another one. If the only thing you keep pulling up when you put your faith line out there is a big catfish with a big head and whiskers popped all over it, drop it back in the water. As a matter of fact, throw the whole rod and reel in and go to another lake. God told Samuel to go to Bethlehem. Sometimes you're in a relationship with a church you've been in for 15 years, and you haven't been getting anything from the services, but you won't leave because it's your grandmother's church. God says, "Go to Bethlehem." The only thing present where you are is the only thing you'll be able to enter into relationship with. Go where God sends you!

Because of our nature and training, we hold on. For instance, when the Emancipation Proclamation was signed and slaves were considered free men and women in spite of President Lincoln signing this document ending the civil war and slavery, there were still people who did not want to leave their master's plantation. God is doing the same thing for you today. He says, "I want you free." Some people look at what they are getting out of their current relationship and miss God saying there is only enough in it to keep you in bondage. What are you looking for? For 15 years, maybe that's all there is in that place.

Trust God to Lead You to Your Bridge

When God begins promoting you, He does so in ways you'll never expect. In His choice of David as king, He did not select the persons Samuel thought should've been crowned because Samuel was looking at their stature, but God was looking into their hearts. We find this situation in I Samuel 16:4-11:

> "And the elders of the town trembled at his coming and said, Comest thou peaceably? And he said, Peaceably. I am come to sacrifice unto the Lord. Sanctify yourselves and come with me to the sacrifice. And he sanctified Jesse and his sons, and called them to the sacrifice. And it came to pass when they were come, that he looked on Eliab and said, Surely, the Lord's anointed is before him . . . ."

Samuel believed Eliab was God's chosen because he looked like he had the potential to be a king. This tells me that without

God's influence, we do not know how to choose people to be in our lives. We don't know how to select friends, mates, or significant others, i.e., business partners. We don't know how to choose relationships with things—from a job to our cars to even picking the color of carpet for our homes. We don't know how to choose relationships with anything or anyone because we have our focus in the wrong direction. You have to trust God to lead you to make the right decision.

> "But the Lord said unto Samuel, Look not on his countenance, nor on the height of his stature; because I have refused him. For the Lord seeth not as man seeth: for man looketh on the outward appearance, but the Lord looketh on the heart. Then Jesse called Abinadab, and made him pass before Samuel. And he said, Neither hath the Lord chosen this." (I Samuel 16:7-9)

I believe Samuel closed his eyes to the natural status of things at that point. After he looked at Eliab and God said, "No, it's not in his appearance," he probably closed his eyes and trusted God to make the selection. It's not in your eyes. It's in what God directs you to do through your heart and His Word. That sounds like relationship, what God directs through the heart. He is the only one who knows the intent and the content of the heart of every individual.

Let's pick up the reading in Verses 11 and 12, "And Jesse made seven of his sons to pass before Samuel. And Samuel said unto Jesse, 'The Lord hath not chosen these.' And Samuel said unto Jesse, 'Are here all thy children?' And he said, 'There remaineth yet the youngest . . . .'" God does not deal with your situations the way you think He will. He will not bless you in the same manner every time. Your blessing may come from the person you least expect. Your blessing may be the man or woman you least expect. However, God knows what is inside of them.

There is a friend of mine who is a minister's daughter. She is very prim, proper. She made it well through school. She is very educated, rather nice looking, and has some good things going for her. Because of who her parents were, she had very high expectations of the man she was to potentially marry, and rightfully so. She wanted her gentlemen callers to be nice looking, suave, smooth, nicely dressed, that sort of thing. Those relationships never worked out for her. Most men were never interested in her because she was a little too "holy" for them. Her father, the minister, was the kind of man who would lay his wrist watch on the coffee table when a young man visited her. At precisely nine o'clock, he would get up, walk in the room, pick up his watch, and put it on his arm. That was her visitor's signal that it was time to get his things and get out of there. There was no such thing as a man taking her somewhere on a date because her father did not believe in movies or dating, so there was really nowhere they could take her.

So this woman got out of the mode of dating and became involved in the things of God. Then she began dating a country fellow. He was as country as cotton. He wore "huckle-buck" shoes. He was the kind of person who wasn't exactly with the rest of the crowd. He wore a blazer that didn't match his shirt or tie, nor did they match his pants. He sported an Afro, but it was "whopped" on one side. He also spoke with a Southern drawl, "Hey, how yawl doin?" Underneath those external flaws, however, he was really a nice-looking guy. He just didn't have anyone to tell him how to dress well.

When I heard she was dating him, I couldn't believe it. I said, "Come on, it's not so, say it isn't so." Then I talked to her and found out it was true. The next time I saw the guy, he had on clothes that matched, a haircut—everything was together. He was still country and still a cowboy. When I spoke with her about her decision to date him, she said, "The first time we went out on a date, I saw his wallet! I realized he had potential." Behind closed doors she revealed to me that she saw how much money he had. As it turned out, he was loaded. His family owned several businesses. He had real estate in the country, cows, chickens, hogs—everything. I mean, he was rolling in it. He had a nice car and could buy a new one, cash money, anytime he was ready. Most of the women didn't see this. They said, "Look at the way he looks." She saw his wallet and said, "That boy is my baby in disguise!" They are still married today. He built her a new house, and they later moved to another one with several acres of land on a lake. Seemingly all he wants to know is what she wants.

I am trying to tell you that sometimes your eyes may deceive you. You don't know what God has for you. It may be tucked away in a place like Peter called "the hidden man of the heart" (I Peter 3:4). It may be way down on the inside, but if you walk with God, He will direct you to the person sanctioned to be with you from the beginning of time, and that person will be a bridge in your life, not a burden. Don't be deceived by outward appearances. I have found that a lot of the time people who boast as if they have a lot of things and are on the move, are just the opposite. Sometimes it's the ones who look as if they have nothing. If you get in a tight spot financially, they are the ones with the financial means to bail you out.

Have you ever had a grandmother like this? She looked as poor as a church mouse, but every time your birthday came, granny would reach around in her bosom to search for money. She didn't reach in there and pull out the first thing, she had to dig deeper and count in order to find the dollar she was going to give you. And she would never let you look. That's the way my paternal grandmother was. It took her a few minutes to say, "Come here, George." I knew it was birthday time. She'd go into her bosom, but it wasn't immediate, she'd have to find it. "Let me see, there were some other things in here." Then she'd come up with the dollar bill she was going to give me. That is the way it is in life. God has some things concealed, and you are not going to get them until you walk with Him and let Him lead you to them.

The future king was concealed from Samuel's natural eyes; he had to allow the Lord to lead him to the person who was going to replace Saul. "And Samuel said unto Jesse, 'Are here all thy children?' And he said, 'There remaineth yet the youngest, and, behold, he keepeth the sheep'" (I Samuel 16:11). A sheep keeper! Now that should tell you something. Do you remember what we read in St. John, Chapter 10? The Lord puts us in relationship with sheep, not hirelings, wolves, or goats. Sheep. Yes, that's the one who is willing to become pliable, flexible; they are teachable and they do not mind following.

"And Samuel said unto Jesse, 'Send and fetch him: for we will not sit down till he comes hither.' And he sent, and brought him in." Now let's read from the Amplified Bible. "Jesse sent and brought him. David had a healthy reddish complexion and beautiful eyes, and was fine looking." The King James Version says, "Now he was ruddy, and withal of a beautiful countenance, and goodly to look to." Really, he was a wild man because he worked in the field. Yet, he was good to look at. He was a blessing. He was a bridge. It didn't appear to be that way at the beginning. And God says to Samuel, "Arise, and anoint him: for this is he" (I Samuel 16:12).

Sanctioned Relationships: an Attraction to Satan

Just as God anointed David to be king, we too must take the same approach in choosing key people to influence our lives. There are some people in your circle of friends who are in your life illegally, because God has not anointed them to be there. They have just attached themselves to you. You see, you have a right to decide who is going to be included in your circle of friends because you are a child of God. You have to approve of them being in your life.

I don't know how you feel about it, but I believe it is a privilege to be my friend. I am not cocky; you too, should see yourself this way. It is a privilege to be your friend because you know what kind of friend you're going to be. Everyone can't attach themselves to me because there are people who act as sponges, and I do not desire that in my life. The Bible even says in the book of Job that God did not turn his affliction until he prayed for his friends (Job 42:10). That's when you sanction people, when they begin to be friends—people who are in relationship with you who you can pray for and who can pray for you. One of the things I want to tell you is that when God selects, He anoints. When God selects and anoints people to be your friends, they become the object of attraction to the enemy. I have seen many people who have experienced God placing the right person in their lives. God anointed someone to clean them up, bring them out, make them who they are, and the devil started talking to them. Have you seen people like this?

I remember when I was in college, there were women who worked two and three jobs to take care of their husbands who could barely work because of the demands of medical school, or some other specialized field of study. All of their attention was focused on finishing their education. The wife worked, and they studied, but when the husband graduated from school he left her. That's wrong! The woman raised him up, blessed him, brought him out, then the adversary started talking to him, saying, "Man, you look all right. You have some money in your pocket now, so why are you there with that beat-down wife?" She's "beat down" because she was bringing her husband up. If supporting him caused her to be in the state she is in, then her husband should bring her up as well.

When God selects and anoints, that person begins to be attractive to Satan and he begins to pull at that individual by talking to them. Remember Adam and Eve? God anointed Adam to be a bridge to Eve, then the couple became attractive to the snake. He began to talk to them, and eventually he talked them out of their salvation, their garden, and their fellowship with the Lord. At the end of it, because the snake talked, because the couple was attractive, because of the anointing of God, they walked out of the garden empty-handed. All that was left was a memory.

I've seen this happen to man after man and woman after woman. God blessed them with a bridge in their life who brought them over, and when they got over they looked back and said, "I don't even know you." However, it's only a matter of time before it catches up with them. They will try to be a bridge to a new person in their life, and when they bring them over, the new person will look back and say, "I don't know you either." It is a vicious cycle. So, when God begins to bless you, don't forget the bridge that brought you over. Don't walk away from God, or your God-ordained bridge.

As a pastor, I have seen people come to church, join, and begin feeding on the Word. They are growing spiritually, their finances are being blessed, their job is being blessed, and their children are blessed. They are happy at their place of worship, but then they have a spouse who tells them they won't attend the church they are being so blessed by. I have seen people pack their things and follow after them saying, "I'm going to be with my spouse!" Do they even belong to a church? God is blessing you and leading you to greener pastures watering your soul, yet you pack up and follow a man or woman who isn't leading you anywhere? It's not God. I have seen both parties end up going nowhere saying, "We're home praying for God to lead us to a church home." How much further out of the Will of God can you get? When God puts you in relationship, please let it be known this day that Satan will start pulling at you. Do you know why? You are attractive to him now. As soon as Samuel declared that David was God's choice, what happened? Satan began to pull at David because God established perfect relationship with him, and out of that fertility and growth, Satan said, "I like what I see, now I want it."

I have seen people leave the church for two or more years, without knowing where to go, in order to further develop their relationship with the Word. They left one church and haven't joined another one. They haven't planted any roots anywhere; they're just looking and traveling. Listen sisters, if your husband is not in the kingdom of God, he cannot lead you to a church that is! He may lead you to one that looks good, but he sure can't lead you to the one that God has chosen and selected for you. He wouldn't know the voice of God if it came to him. For you to follow that is to take your life into your own hands.

Do you know what else I have seen? I have seen people in a church walk with God and do fine. They have been a blessing to the ministry and the ministry has been a blessing to them. Then they meet a woman or a man and say, "I have to go with my friend." Where was your friend when you needed them? "They didn't have what I needed." If in fact God has placed you in a church, you have to protect that relationship because it is going to lead you to the proper adjustment and assessment of all other relationships you'll have. When you go in the wrong direction in your relationship with God, you will miss it everywhere else. I have seen people go along with a seemingly "perfect" person they liked so much, follow them around, and jump from church to church. They never get back into a fresh relationship with God, and the fertility and blessings of God never come back to them again. Why? They made the wrong decision. When God sets you in relationship, you have to know that Satan is going to pull at you to try to get you away from it, because that is where your blessing is.

God and His way always leads to a bridging effect. The very nature of God and all He sends is to elevate us to a higher plane of living. St. John 10:10 speaks about these bridging qualities. "The thief (Satan, a burden) cometh . . . I, Jesus (the bridge) am come that you may have life. . . ." The Amplified Version of this passage says of our Heavenly Father's intent, ". . . Life filled to the full." Satan is the ultimate burden, as evidenced by this verse of scripture. Therefore, he and all his associates can only further burden us by attempting to kill, steal, kill, and destroy.

CHAPTER 7

How It All Started

A relationship, in short, is how people are connected. The connection of people for accomplishments is the real reason for any type of relationship. The key to peak performance in any arena is making correct and meaningful connections. I am increasingly becoming more aware of the fact that all that is to be created, made, developed, earned, and accomplished will only be capacitated through relationships. This fact makes gaining an understanding in this subject paramount. In Proverbs 4:7, the word of the Lord states, "Wisdom is the principal thing; therefore get wisdom: and with all thy getting get understanding." Verse 13 of the same chapter says, "Take fast hold of instruction: let her not go: keep her; for she is thy life." These two scriptures clearly show the need for wisdom and instruction in every area of life, as well as in relationships. A relationship is the God-inspired method in which the human race receives everything from Him. God is the giver, and He gives through people. Notice St. Luke 6:38, "Give, and it will be given unto you; good measure, pressed down, and shaken together, and running over, will men give into your bosom." How did God promise to give to His children? Through a relationship with people returning back the harvest from the seed planted. Without correct credence and appreciation for this process of God's dealing with man, it could be easy to see how one could not receive something, although it was being sent directly to him.

Even in the case of Abraham, known as the father of the faithful, God said to him in Genesis 12:1-3, "Now the Lord had said unto Abram (this was his name before receiving the promise), Get thee out of thy country, and from thy kindred, and from thy father's house, unto a land that I will show thee: And I will make of thee a great nation, and I will bless thee, and make thy name great; and thou shall be a blessing: And I will bless them that bless thee, and curse him that curseth thee: and in thee shall all the earth be blessed." In the midst of God initiating His covenant to Abraham, He shows that this covenant of blessing would only be transferred "in thee." This denotes relationship as the principle being used to serve as the conduit for partaking of the blessing.

In this vein, it is important to note that Lot, Abraham's nephew— (relationship), became amazingly wealthy because of his association with the one who had the blessing (Genesis 13:1-6). Note that this all took place in spite of the fact that Lot was not included in God's initial instructions to Abraham. In fact, Abraham was directed to get away from his kindred. Exodus 3:6 gives us insight into what took place during Moses' encounter with God on the backside of Mt. Horeb. It states, "Moreover He said, I am the God of thy father, the God of Abraham, the God of Isaac, the God of Jacob . . . ." This verse has some very important elements in it. First, as God introduced Himself to Moses, He said, "I am the God of your father." This means that God was in relationship with Moses because of the relationship with his father Amram. Second, God mentions a tribal succession that includes the great patriarchs of the Bible—Abraham, Isaac, and Jacob. God essentially was saying that whatever was going to be done for the children of Israel through Moses would be accomplished as a result of relationship.

The truth of the matter is that our God is revealed through relationship. The Bible is a book of relationship. It details the relationship of a loving Father with His children. Our relationships are to be patterns of how God passes His good gifts to His family through inheritance. Notice Romans 8:14-17, "For as many as are led by the Spirit of God, they are the sons of God. For ye have not received the spirit of bondage again to fear; but ye have received the Spirit of adoption, whereby we cry, Abba, Father. The Spirit itself (Himself) beareth witness with our spirit, that we are the children of God. And if children, then heirs, heirs of God, and joint-heirs with Christ; if so be that we suffer with Him, that we might be glorified together." This passage of scripture indicates that through relationship as heirs we inherit God's best for our lives.

Satan's Attack on God's Purpose

God is purposeful in all He does. The Old Testament book of Isaiah 45:18 states: "For thus saith the Lord that created the heavens; God Himself that formed the earth and made it; He hath established it; He created it not in vain, He formed it to be inhabited: I am the Lord; and there is none else." Despite the fact that the book of Genesis opens with the planet being submerged in water because of Satan's betrayal of his relationship with God and subsequent fall into the earth, the earth and everything contained therein was designed to function within the lines of God's designed purpose. Satan always attempts to destroy or at the very least pervert God's purpose. We understand this purpose from the beginning was to create a man to walk in perfect relationship with Him and therefore receive His highest. Contrary to this plan, Satan walked into the Garden of Eden in the body of a serpent (Genesis 3) and through subtlety deceived man out of his relationship with the Father. Satan has the mind-set of this kind of destruction because he knows the benefits that can come to us through healthy relationships, especially with God our heavenly Father. Satan is aware of the power of God released through relationships, as he was guardian of the very throne of God. If this is true, then how did he lose this glorious position? Isaiah 14:12-19 says, "How are thou fallen from heaven, O Lucifer, son of the morning! How art thou cut down to the ground, which didst weaken the nations! For thou hast said in thine heart, I will ascend into heaven, I will exalt my throne above the stars of God: I will sit also upon the mount of the congregation, in the sides of the north: I will ascend above the heights of the clouds: I will be like the most High. Yet thou shalt be brought down to hell, to the sides of the pit. They that shall see thee shall narrowly look upon thee, and consider thee, saying, is this the man that made the earth to tremble, that did shake kingdoms; that made the world as a wilderness, and destroyed the cities thereof; that opened not the house of the prisoners?" Notice the phrases, "didst weaken the nations," in Verse 12 and "made the earth to tremble, that did shake kingdoms" in Verse 16. These two verses indicate that Satan, the lawless one, was and always will be concerned with the destruction of humanity through his diabolical intervention in relationships. Just think of it—from cures of sickness and disease to undiscovered technological breakthroughs—all God has intended for the construction of societies can be enhanced and advanced through the building of successful relationships.

Qualifying for the Armor of Protection on Relationships

In keeping with all that has been said, I would like to turn your attention to the New Testament book of Ephesians. In each chapter, the writer, St. Paul the Apostle, discusses the different facets of relationships. In Chapter 1, the theme is the believer's relationship with immeasurable blessings available through Christ. Chapter 2 discusses the relationship between Christ and His Holy church. Chapter 3 introduces the relationship between the author of the book of Ephesians and the Gentile church. Chapter 4 discloses our relationship with the Holy Spirit producing unity. Chapter 5 reveals the relationship between light and darkness and God's order for the family. Chapter 6, verses 1-9, opens with a continuation of the discussion on family and servant relationships. However, in verse 10 we find these significant words, "Finally, my brethren, be strong in the Lord, and in the power of His might." The word "finally" is used here to denote the instructions given regarding relationships in each of the previous chapters. The thought here is that the relationships spoken of in chapters 1-6 must first be properly ordered and maintained. This further qualifies us for the benefit of wearing the whole armor of God (Ephesians 6:11). This armor is our protection from all of the wiles or trickery and strategies of our enemy, Satan. The reason more believers do not receive this promised protection is found in the failure to understand the importance of correctly assessing and placing sufficient effort in the perfection of these relationships. Let's examine this word "finally" more closely. The challenge here is in knowing that the benefits will not be realized until the things of the previous chapters are completed first. Notice the usage of the term "brethren." This is a relationship word. A great key is being exposed in this text. I think we can safely draw the conclusion that perfecting the relationships referred to in the aforementioned chapters potentially brings us into brotherhood with Jesus and an entitlement to wear His armor. This "brotherhood" entitles the bearer thereof to become a fellow partner and partaker of all that Christ has and is (Romans 8:17). This also reveals Satan's reasoning for fighting godly relationships. The enemy desires to have all people with whom we interact to occupy wrong capacities, causing our brotherhood with Jesus not to occur and consequently forfeiting our right to the inheritance the Father has promised.

CHAPTER 8

Loyalty

====================

In this chapter, I would like to discuss one of the most important factors in determining the fitness of others to occupy significant capacities in your life. There is a very meaningful word which is rarely discussed in the Western Hemisphere. It is the word *loyalty*. A comprehensive understanding of this word can heave a greater leverage in the arena of people skills. The word loyalty in its common definition means showing faithfulness to one's family, friends, ideals, business associations, country, etc.

From this definition, we can determine that the word loyalty is a relationship term. A better definition of this word loyalty is "a commitment to someone or something without regard to one's welfare or well-being." In order to grasp the full meaning of these terms, let's also define the word "faithful." This is a synonym for the word loyalty which means, "sincere; honest; reliable; or having complete trust or confidence; an unquestioning belief."

The true test of an individual's readiness to fulfill certain requirements and various capacities, is their willingness to modify themselves and their schedules to accommodate reasonable requests, whether communicated or interpreted. Consider this scenario. An individual is hired and shortly thereafter is requested to work an extra day outside of their normal work schedule, and their response to this dilemma is, "I have already made plans to go shopping and therefore cannot come in." Chances are good that the planned shopping excursion is something that is not life-threatening and can be rescheduled relatively easily. This individual's unwillingness to demonstrate good judgment and prudence in this matter, in my opinion, proves their disloyalty to the employer. In many people's minds this would be an insignificant matter and should be ignored. However, it should serve as a flashing neon light in terms of predicting their future devotion or dedication. This same means of evaluation can be used to measure the future direction of any relationship. Whatever one is unwilling to defer for another is evidence of a lack of proper appreciation for the thing being sacrificed. This principle is supported by the Word of God; after all, it was a choice of whom we would enjoy relationship with and a denunciation of the other which resulted in our being born into the family of God. In St. Matthew 6:24, Jesus explained, "No man can serve two masters: for either he will hate the one, and love the other; or else he will hold to the one, and despise the other. You cannot serve God and mammon." This admonition should serve as case in point to illustrate the fact that loyalty or faithfulness begins with a choice to elevate one over the other. Remember our base definition involves making something or someone superior to the other without regard to one's personal welfare or well-being. To detect true motives, sometimes asking those vying for significant positions in your life to accommodate last minute and inopportune pleas can in many instances locate the true level of their commitment, or the lack thereof.

The Loyalty Test

The Holy Scriptures have a lot to say on the subject of loyalty. The wording more commonly used is "faithful." Any person in any type of relationship should become familiar with what I call the three tests of faithfulness/loyalty. Notice St. Luke 16:10-12, "He that is faithful (loyal) in that which is least is faithful (loyal) also in much: and he that is unjust in the least is unjust also in the much. If therefore you have not been faithful (loyal) in the unrighteous mammon (money or riches which are neither good nor evil in and of itself), who will commit to your trust the true riches (the anointing)?

And if ye have not been faithful (loyal) in that which is another man's, who will give you that which is your own?" So, as you can see, the loyalty test is threefold. It consists of loyalty or faithfulness in the areas of that which is said to be least—matters concerning money and the anointing—and that which belongs to another.

Proverbs 11:13 provides another view on this subject of loyalty or faithfulness, "A talebearer (whisperer or gossip) revealeth secrets: but he that is of a faithful (loyal) spirit concealeth (covers) the matter." This is a very important truth. Evidence which proves loyalty in an unmistakable way can be seen in how private information is guarded or protected. This scripture reference is not suggesting that loyalty is conspiracy, but rather is an issue of discretion that should cause the loyal one to be very cautious about the handling of private data. When a person is more concerned with the exposure of trusted information rather than the protection of the same, it is essentially a lack of faithfulness in that which belongs to another. As you can see, the loyalty test always works. Disloyalty always falls into one of these three categories.

Exposing something which was divulged in secret is a break from our working definition of loyalty, which dictates a consistent commitment to something or someone without regard to one's well-being or welfare. Generally speaking, if someone cannot be trusted to control their tongue, neither should they be trusted with their actions. There is a distinct correlation between what the mouth says and the body does reciprocally. Psalm 39:1 says, "I said I will take heed to my ways, that I sin not with my tongue . . . ." Ecclesiastes 5:6 demonstrates the same point, "Suffer not thy mouth to cause thy flesh to sin; neither say thou before the angel, that it was an error: wherefore should God be angry at thy voice and destroy the work of thy hands?" The tongue always will navigate the direction of the body's actions, therefore when the mouth proves disloyal, it is only a matter of time before this disloyalty manifests itself in behavior. A bridge is loyal and can be entrusted with esoteric situations.

Common Characteristics of Bridges (or Loyal Persons)

There are certain commonalities that loyal persons (bridges) share. A loyal person (bridge) will remove burdens instead of causing them. Isaiah 10:27 says, " And it shall come to pass in that day, that his burden shall be taken away from off thy shoulder, and his yoke from off thy neck, and the yoke shall be destroyed because of the anointing." Loyalty in and of itself is a bridge because of its rarity if nothing else. I would like to submit two scriptures to validate this point: Psalm 12:1, "Help, Lord; for the godly man ceaseth; for the faithful (loyal) fail from among the children of men," and Proverbs 20:6, "Most men will proclaim everyone his own goodness: but a faithful (loyal) man who can find?" Are you a loyal or faithful person? Can you be trusted with the deepest, darkest secrets of another?

Successful relationships are constructed by loyal persons whose loyalty is determined by the words they speak. Let's now refer to Proverbs 18:4, "The words of a man's mouth are as deep waters, and the wellspring of wisdom as a flowing brook." This passage describes the effect of words on the human sphere of existence. Words are containers of thoughts and images which develop the psyche. When a bridge enters into a scenario, their loyalty is immediately obvious because of the quality of words they speak. An individual who is "bridge-minded" is watchful to ensure their words are never spoken out of duplicity. In Chapter 20 of this same book of the Bible, Verse 5, the author, King Solomon, further states, "Counsel in the heart of a man is like deep water; but a man of understanding (a bridge) will draw it out." This conglomeration of words simply means that a loyal person also is a person of understanding or wisdom. This wise person actually chooses to see the object of the loyalty differently from all others so as to motivate them toward releasing words that build up rather than tear down. This is true whether they are persons who are laconic or tend to be long-winded. Legend has it that even in the life of former world heavyweight champion Muhammad Ali, the value of such a person was evident. It seems that there was a man by the name of Drew "Boudini" Brown whose job in being a constant companion to the champion was to affirm with a consistent flow of pleasant, loyal, and kind words just how great "the greatest" actually was. He is credited with writing the poem, "Float like a butterfly, sting like a bee." There is a lot to be said for those who through their skillful usage of words bring out the best in others.

The New Testament book of I Corinthians 13:11 is a good staple for insight into the structure for determining what loyalty is. "When I was a child, I spake as a child, I understood as a child, I thought as a child: but when I became a man, I put away childish things." The placement of the colon in this text is interesting. Notice the colon is after the statements regarding childishness, followed by the statement about becoming a man or entering into adulthood. Keep in mind that normally in the punctuation aspect of the English language, whatever comes after the colon explains the statement in front of it. This helps us with understanding the significance of this text as it relates to loyalty. In order for one to be called mature, or thus loyal, there must be the putting away of childish or petty things. As long as there are people, there always will be the circumstantial opportunity for offense. A loyal person will discover ways to put it far from them so that the relationship is unhindered.

Jesus made the much-quoted statement in St. John 8:32, "And you shall know the truth, and the truth shall make you free." In this colossal, foundational text, upon first reading, seems to imply that coming in contact with any and all truth will emancipate the hearer thereof from weight, constrictions, or limitations. I believe this suggestion is not incorrect but rather incomplete. The word "know" is used to raise the idea that truth in and of itself will not make one free, but rather "known" or understood truth does. The word "know" is more substantive than simply hearing or having read about a person. To know means to be well-informed of, to be sure of, or have an intimate relationship with or about. This verse of scripture is actually speaking about a relationship with the truth. It might better be translated, "And you must get to know Jesus Christ (the truth), and through your relationship with Him and knowledge of Him, you shall be made free from every encumbrance." So you see it is a loyal ongoing relationship with the King of kings and Lord of lords that is responsible for producing the insight and revelation necessary to evolve into a bridge instead of being a burden. This same relationship with Jesus also is responsible for successfully detecting bridges and burdens alike. May all you do forever connect you with the bridge of God's grace, assisting your detour from the burden of satanic onslaughts.

Confession

Heavenly Father, thank you for your love for me. I am convinced of your love. You gave Your Son Jesus Christ to die as the payment for all my sins. Through His suffering and death, I now have a legal right to receive forgiveness for of all my actions against You. Romans 10:8-10 states that You (the Word) are close to me, affecting my mouth and mind so that I can believe and say that Jesus actually died to represent me; and that by my believing and saying this truth, I will be saved. Therefore, as an act of my will and of my faith, I say that Satan no longer is in control of my life. Jesus is my Savior and Lord. I hereby make this affirmation of my faith in Christ, by saying I am saved, I am saved, I am saved. Now that I am in Your family heavenly Father, I receive Your words of life that bring insight and illumination to every instance I am confronted with. I worship You through Your Word. Thank You for bringing me to the place of perfect knowledge of the Truth, so that I am able to take charge of every instance that involves my circle of family, friends, business associates, and partners, in each level of my life, in Jesus' name, Amen.

APPENDIX

Answers to Frequently Asked Questions

This information is designed specially to provide scriptural answers to frequently asked questions regarding interpersonal relationships. However, before presenting the questions, I would like to explain the spiritual forum I've used to arrive at these responses. I advise that you use the same methods to tap into the wisdom of God for your every need.

I John 2:20 states, "But ye have an unction from the Holy One, and ye know all things." This scripture means believers do not have to wait until we get into situations before we know if they will work out or not. You don't have to wait to get into a bad relationship or business deal before you know it's bad. You don't have to hire the wrong person before evidence proves you made a mistake. You should begin to trust and rely upon the unction of the Holy One, who will reveal all things. This unction is an inner witness or voice that leads you to a thing or away from it before you actually have "hands-on" experience. Sometimes "hands-on" experience can be costly. It can cost you your life, your light, your willingness to thrive and survive. So begin relying on the inner witness (voice) of the Holy Spirit as you choose your relationships.

Let's parallel this scripture with Isaiah 11:1-3:

> "And there shall come forth a rod (or an extension) out of the stem of Jesse, and a Branch shall grow out of his roots: And the spirit of the Lord shall rest upon him, the spirit of wisdom and understanding, the spirit of counsel and might, the spirit of knowledge and of the fear of the Lord; And shall make him of quick understanding in the fear of the Lord: and he shall not judge after the sight of his eyes, neither reprove after the hearing of his ears."

The "Spirit of the Lord" in the book of Isaiah is the same force as the unction described in I John 2:20. That force is called the anointing of God. This anointing rested upon Jesus, giving Him quick understanding, a keen sense of discernment, and the ability to know all things. We have this same anointing on the inside of us to help us make sound decisions. So, before you make any major decision in your life, I challenge you to pay close attention to the unction you've received from the Holy Spirit and you will know what choices to make. Jesus rested upon this anointing, and you can as well.

Now that you understand the Holy Spirit's ability to provide answers and directions, please receive the answers provided below that were given to me by the anointing to know all things.

Question #1
Why does a person lose interest in their spouse or any other person in whom they have established relationship?

Many things can cause this, including time, age, affliction, discouragement, disappointment, or dissatisfaction. Sometimes the opposite other is the object of one's discontentment. My advice is to use faith to redeem your interest as you would use faith to receive anything else. Faith is saying or agreeing with the Word of God. II Corinthians 5:7 says, "For we walk by faith, not by sight." Do not walk by what you see, in this case, a lack of interest. Confess the following scriptures and don't be moved to doubt and unbelief by your present set of circumstances: I Corinthians 13:1 (Interject "My spouse and I", or whatever the case may be, as the subject of each confession) and Joel 2:25-26. Use faith and confessions to redeem any time you've lost in your relationship.

Question #2

What are the pros and cons of spouses attending different places of worship?

God's mind-set always has been centered around unity and oneness. Unity is the place of consistent, directional agreement. Oneness is the position of all involved persons working together to accomplish unity. St. Matthew 12:25 says, "every city or house divided against itself shall not stand." I Corinthians 10:1-5 recounts the exodus of God's chosen people, the Israelites. They ate the same spiritual food and drank the same spiritual drink, "for they drank of that spiritual Rock that followed them: and that Rock was Christ." God's whole emphasis in this scripture is that people in relationship with Him should eat from the same table. You may be attending good churches, but it is difficult for two people to eat from different spiritual tables and grow the same. Both pastors will see certain scriptures a little differently, and if both spouses take their church's teachings seriously as they should, and bring them into the home, it will be grounds for division. Begin to use your faith to believe that God will unite you, as a couple, in the church He desires you to attend.

Confession: "My spouse and I are eating the same spiritual food and drinking the same spiritual drink, thereby we're growing together faithfully in the things of God."

Question #3

My relationship with my spouse and children is troubled. Where and how do I begin to correct this?

Start with self change, and the rest of your family will follow. St. Luke 6:31 says, "And as ye would that men should to you, do ye also to them likewise." Whatever you want to see others emulate, you set it forth as an example.

Question #4

I've been married for more than 10 years. I recently have been born-again. Although I am growing in positive ways, my spouse and children are pulling away. As a result, I have become tired and my spouse is miserable. Where do I begin making the necessary changes?

I Corinthians 7:12 reads, "If any brother hath a wife that believeth not, and she be pleased to dwell with him, let him not put her away." The same instruction applies to the woman in Verse 13, which follows. If your spouse chooses to remain married to you, let him or her remain without "preaching" to them all of the time. Instead, live the life of a true believer. Attend church regularly and arrive home in a timely manner, read your Bible, pray, and make daily confessions and your spouse will be persuaded by your consistent actions. "For what knowest thou, O wife, whether thou shalt save thy husband? Or how knowest thou, O man, whether thou shalt save thy wife?" (I Corinthians 7:16). For more information on this subject, refer to Chapter 4 of this book.

Question #5

I have a good friend whose child is very spoiled. Even though this child talks back and has temper tantrums, no form of discipline is being used by the parents or by my friend's in-laws. How do I tell my friend that their child needs discipline?

Let's examine three scriptures to receive God's mind-set in the area of disciplining children:

a. Psalm 127:3—"Lo, children are an heritage of the Lord . . . ."
b. Proverbs 22:15— "Foolishness is bound in the heart of a child; but the rod of correction shall drive it far from him."
c. Proverbs 23:13-14—"Withhold not correction from the child: for if thou beatest him with the rod, he shall not die. Thou shalt beat him with the rod, and shalt deliver his soul from hell."

We must first recognize that God has perfect knowledge. Since the concept of reproduction and children originated from Him, and He is a perfect Father, it is safe to conclude that He knows best how to develop and nurture them so they will grow into productive adults. The "rod of correction" should be used when children are very young and in their formative process. In the early years of their lives, children have not begun to process information with rational thinking. They usually do things on impulse without considering the consequences. The rod of correction will guide them on what they should and should not do. However, as they grow, and begin to think situations through more soundly, parents can begin using words to guide and direct their children. As God leads, information of this nature can be shared if the recipients are open. If they are not open now, as time and experience progress they may become very open to these instructions!

Question #6

My spouse and I sleep in separate beds. We are young adults, what advice do you have for our situation?

Discover the true nature of your problem and repair it. Genesis 2:24 says "Therefore shall a man leave his father and his mother, and shall cleave unto his wife . . . ." You've left your parents to cleave unto one another. Sadly, there are some major unresolved situations involved in this relationship. If you are experiencing this, my advice is to seek spiritual counseling from a spirit-filled, qualified, non-biased third party.

Question #7

My spouse and I are "babes in Christ," but my spouse continues to maintain relationships with unsaved friends?How do I handle this situation?

Be consistent in sowing the seed of what you want to see in your spouse. (St. Luke 6:31) If you desire your spouse to sever friendships with unsaved friends so he or she can grow deeper into the things of God, then take the initiative to sever your friendships of this kind. What you do not want to do is harass your spouse. He or she will surely withdraw from you when you come into their presence. You'll be thought of as someone who badgers, complains, and makes things difficult and hard. Instead of being a bridge, you'll become a burden. My advice is to read Proverbs 19:13; 21:9,19; 25:24; and 27:15. These scriptures describe one's reactions to a contentious person—they are driven further away. Then trust the Holy Spirit to bring about the necessary convictions to allow for appropriate changes to occur. (St. John 14:26;16:13)

Question #8

Is oral sex a sin?

Sin is defined as "missing the mark" of God's standards set forth by His word (the Bible). In order for an act to be categorized as "sin," there must be a definite, clear, direct word from God establishing the "mark" on a matter. Such a scripture does not exist, to my knowledge. Keep in mind, there are some actions not classified as "sin," but could qualify as "weights." (Hebrews 12:1) "Marriage is honorable in all, and the bed undefiled . . . ." (Hebrews 13:4) Any type of sexual activity between a husband and wife should be determined by them only. The Bible is silent on the specifics. There must, however, be consent or agreement. If force is used, then the issue turns into one of control and God is opposed to this.

Question #9

In a marriage, why is it the woman's responsibility to cook?

It isn't, necessarily. All domestic responsibilities should be *shared* if both spouses work outside the home. If a wife is helping her husband pay bills, her husband should help her with household duties. However, God's desire is for the man to work outside the home while the wife keeps the home. (Genesis 2:7-9,18; Psalm 128:3; Proverbs 12:4) If you are a working spouse and your mate does not assist you around the house, my advice is to mention it only once or twice, confess the Word of God, pray, and practice what you want to see.

Question #10

Do you think a long-distance romantic relationship will work? If not, how can I make it work?

The first thing you should ask yourself is, "What has God said?" Did He say it would work? If He did or did not, He will "uphold all things by the word of his power." (Hebrews 1:3) He hastens His Word to perform it. (Jeremiah 1:12) Therefore, you do not have to concern yourself with trying to make the relationship happen. If He says your relationship will work, it will work.

Question #11

How do I deal with a spouse who brushes off or acts as if they do not understand my attempts to discuss serious issues that pertain to family or to our relationship? They either respond with sarcasm, or never give a straight answer.

Please, do not push the issue with your spouse. As I mentioned before, (refer to Question #9), many people do not respond in the way you would like if they repeatedly are criticized. In fact, many of them shut down, closing themselves off from communicating with you. Only the Holy Spirit can convince a person to change. He knows how to reach and touch people in ways you cannot. St. John 14:26 and St. John 16:7-13 support my answer.

Question #12

What do I do when my mate is spending time with others and putting them before me? This mate also points out my faults yet they are unwilling to see their own.

As I previously have suggested, sow the seeds of change. (St. Luke 6:31) Model the behavior you want to see in your spouse. Also, give your mate time and space so that attraction for you can return. Perhaps you have been so preoccupied with the faults of your significant other person that you have neglected other interests in your life. I advise you to spend time developing yourself. Taking up a hobby may give both of you space and time to grow.

Question #13

My child is born-again, but is living with someone without being married to them. How do I minister to both of them without condemning them?

Love them unconditionally. I Corinthians 13:8 says charity (agape love) never fails. Love gets the job done. It always will work. However, if the Spirit of God leads you to address their relationship, do so. Hebrews 12:5-14 discusses the benefit of chastisement. Let your son or daughter and their companion know you love them unreservedly even though the Word of God does not agree with their living situation.

Question #14
Should a wife always be willing to submit to her husband sexually, even when she does not feel like it?

I Corinthians 7:3-4 says, "Let the husband *render* unto the wife *due benevolence*: and likewise also the wife unto the husband. The wife hath not power of her own body, but the husband: and likewise also the husband hath not power of his own body, but the wife."

Let's start by defining the italicized words:

Render: To give what is due or correct; to make it available. Make yourself readily available for your spouse.
Due: Fitting or appropriate.
Benevolence: A tendency to do kind or charitable acts.

When we enter these definitions into the scripture, it reads, "Make available to your spouse appropriate kindness or charitable acts." Marriage is not a "by feeling relationship," but a "by faith relationship." Perhaps you may need to communicate with your spouse any dissatisfaction you have in this particular area and suggest solutions to remedy the problems.

Question #15
How can I remain encouraged when I am a single parent and raising my children according to the Word of God, and they continue to cause me heartache and disappointment, sometimes on a daily

basis? How do I keep going even though I am seeing absolutely no fruit?

You are attempting to walk by sight, but the Christian walk is one of faith (II Corinthians 5:7). The key to breakthrough is consistency in the frequency and methods by which you discipline your children, and in speaking the Word of God to and over them. Do not be moved by what you see. St. Mark 11:23, and Hebrews 3:1, 4:14, and 10:23 provide guidance in this area. Refer to the following passages to discover the benefits of diligence and consistency: Exodus 15:26; Deuteronomy 28:1; Proverbs 10:4; 12:24; 13:4.

Question #16

How do I determine if my significant other loves me as much as they love themselves?

In Ephesians 5:28-30, the Bible says that a man should love his wife as he loves himself. You will know if someone loves you if they give to, nourish, and cherish you. If he or she gives relentlessly to you; nourishes or encourages your good traits and qualities by speaking the truth in love, and cherishes or loves and protects your right to have your own thoughts, feelings, and selections, then that person loves you. Refer to Chapter 2's subtitle "Agape Love: A Key Ingredient in Godly Relationships" for more insight on this subject.

When you want to know more about:

- Excellence
- Faith
- Prosperity
- Marriage & Family
- Personal Growth & Development

Then we have a series of teaching tapes that have all the answers you've been searching for. Please call or write us at:

George Matthews Ministries
P.O. Box 360264
Birmingham, AL 35236
(205) 425-4735

Or you can visit us on the World Wide Web at www.nlim.org.